# Genocide since 1945

D0907896

In 1948, three years after the Holocaust came to an end, the United Nations passed the Genocide Convention. The international community was now obligated to prevent or halt what had hitherto, in Winston Churchill's words, been a 'crime without a name', and to punish the perpetrators. Since then, however, genocide has recurred repeatedly. Millions of people have been murdered with impunity inside their own borders by sovereign nation states, largely undeterred by the Convention.

This book traces the history of genocide since 1945. It analyses a number of cases across continents and decades, looking at different explanations for why it has happened and so often. It discusses a range of key issues, including:

- how and why the concept of genocide was developed
- what the Convention defines as genocide
- why it is said to be 'the crime of crimes'
- how genocides happen and the different roles and responses of perpetrators, bystanders, victims and rescuers
- the different stages that genocides go through
- whether anything can or should be done to prevent or halt genocide – the question of 'humanitarian intervention'
- what happens or should happen after genocide – to perpetrators, to survivors and to the societies which have experienced it.

*Genocide since 1945* aims to help the reader understand how, when, where and why this crime has been committed since 1945, why it has proven so difficult to halt or prevent its recurrence and what now might be done about it. It is essential reading for all those interested in the contemporary world.

**Philip Spencer** is Professor in Holocaust and Genocide Studies at Kingston University, UK. His publications include *Nationalism: A Critical Introduction* (2002) with H. Wollman, and *Nationalism: A Reader* (2005) edited with H. Wollman.

# The Making of the Contemporary World
Edited by Eric J. Evans and Ruth Henig

The Making of the Contemporary World series provides challenging interpretations of contemporary issues and debates within strongly defined historical frameworks. The range of the series is global, with each volume drawing together material from a range of disciplines – including economics, politics and sociology. The books in this series present compact, indispensable introductions for students studying the modern world.

# Genocide since 1945

## Philip Spencer

Routledge
Taylor & Francis Group

LONDON AND NEW YORK

First published 2012
by Routledge
2 Park Square, Milton Park, Abingdon, Oxon OX14 4RN

Simultaneously published in the USA and Canada
by Routledge
711 Third Avenue, New York, NY 10017

*Routledge is an imprint of the Taylor & Francis Group, an informa
business*

*British Library Cataloguing in Publication Data*
A catalogue record for this book is available from the British
Library

*Library of Congress Cataloging in Publication Data*
Spencer, Philip.
Genocide since 1945 / Philip Spencer.
p. cm. – (The making of the contemporary world)
1. Genocide. 2. Crimes against humanity. I. Title.
HV6322.7.S655 2012
364.15'1 – dc23
2011049495

ISBN: 978-0-415-60633-2 (hbk)
ISBN: 978-0-415-60634-9 (pbk)
ISBN: 978-0-203-11504-6 (ebk)

Typeset in Times New Roman
by Taylor & Francis Books

MIX
Paper from
responsible sources
FSC
www.fsc.org  FSC® C004839

Printed and bound in Great Britain by the MPG Books Group

# Contents

# Acknowledgements

I have been helped by a number of people in the course of writing this book. I am grateful to Ben Barkow, the Director of the Wiener Library for the Study of the Holocaust and Genocide, for his constant interest in this project. I would like to thank also the British Academy for funding the research conference we organised together, where some of the ideas in this book were presented and discussed. I have benefitted greatly from discussions at various times with Jacques Sémelin, Martin Shaw, Omer Bartov, Gregory Stanton, Andrea Bartoli, Alex Hinton, Daniel Feierstein, Linda Melvern and Marko Hoare, as well as with several other colleagues at conferences of the International Association of Genocide Scholars (IAGS). I am grateful too to Brian Brivati with whom I first started teaching about genocide, and to Marcello Flores who helped me develop our joint European Master's course in Genocide Studies. I would also like to thank my other colleagues on that programme, Jadwiga Koralewicz, Gerard Rowe and Carmen Thiele, as well as Thomas Brudholm and Paul Levine. I should like to thank especially all the students who have taken my courses on the Holocaust and on the Politics of Mass Murder. It was entirely counter-intuitive that so many would want to come and take these courses, and I have greatly appreciated their enthusiasm, commitment and engagement. It is sometimes said that students today are too instrumental. My experience has been exactly the opposite.

I should like also to thank Laura Mothersole and Eve Setch for their enthusiasm and support for this project from the beginning, and Cathy Hurren for her care and attention with the manuscript.

Lastly, my greatest debt is to my family, to Jane, Rosa and Reuben, for all those discussions around the kitchen table, and for their constant love and support.

The Publisher would like to thank David Higham Associates, Yale University Press, Susanne Jonas, Ed McCaughan and Elizabeth

Sutherland Martinez, the Center of Halabja Against Anfalization and Genocide of the Kurds, African Rights, Associated Press and Michael Miller.

While every effort has been made to trace and acknowledge ownership of copyright material used in this volume, the Publishers will be glad to make suitable arrangements with any copyright holders whom it has not been possible to contact.

# Chronology

*This is a list of a number of important events in the history of genocide since 1945. It is not intended as either exhaustive or definitive. A number of genocides are listed, not all of which are accepted as such for various reasons discussed in the course of this book. Some other cases of mass killing, however, are also listed here which could also be classified as genocide, depending on the definition adopted. Estimates for the numbers of victims often vary markedly (for further details, see also Table 2.1 on p.19).*

| | |
|---|---|
| 1945 | January: liberation of Auschwitz by the Soviet Red Army |
| | May: German surrender brings Holocaust to an end |
| 1945–46 | Nuremburg War Crimes Trials |
| 1948 | 9 December Genocide Convention adopted by the UN; 10 December Universal Declaration of Human Rights adopted by the UN |
| 1948 | Start of the Cold War |
| 1951 | Geneva Convention comes into force |
| 1958–61 | 'Great Leap Forward' economic policy in China, attempting rapid industrialisation; mass starvation ensues |
| 1961 | Eichmann trial in Jerusalem |
| 1965–66 | Genocide in Indonesia (see Chapter 4) |
| 1966–69 | Genocide in Biafra, as Nigerian state crushes secession attempt |
| 1966–67 | 'Great Proletarian Cultural Revolution' in China |
| 1965–68 | American combat troops sent to Vietnam; United States drops *c*.3 million tons of bombs: *c*.2 million victims (over 40 per cent civilians) |
| 1969–73 | US bombs Cambodia: *c*.150,000 victims |
| 1971–79 | Idi Amin's regime in Uganda |
| 1971 | Genocide in East Pakistan/Bangladesh (see Chapter 4) |
| 1972 | Genocide of Hutus in Burundi |
| 1974 | Genocide of Guayaki Ache Indians in Paraguay |

| | |
|---|---|
| 1977–78 | 'Red Terror' by ruling Dergue communists; former President Mengistu is indicted *in absentia* for genocide in 1994 in 2006 |
| 1975 | Indonesia invades East Timor |
| 1975–79 | Genocide in Cambodia (see Chapter 4) |
| 1976–83 | Military coup in Argentina and 'Dirty War' by military junta against guerrillas |
| 1980–92 | Civil war in El Salvador |
| 1982 | Mass killing of Sunni Muslims in Hama by Syrian state |
| 1982–83 | Genocide in Guatemala (see Chapter 5) |
| 1983 | Sudan civil war starts |
| 1983–2009 | Sri Lanka – Sinhalese government war with Tamil Tigers; ends with mass killings of Tamils in the last few months on a thin strip of land in the far north of the island |
| 1986 | US finally agrees to ratify Geneva Convention |
| 1987–88 | Genocide of the Kurds in Iraq (see Chapter 6) |
| 1989–91 | Collapse of communism in Eastern Europe and the Soviet Union; end of the Cold War |
| 1992–95 | Genocide in Bosnia; July 1995 Srebrenica massacre (see Chapter 6) |
| 1993 | UN Security Council creates International Criminal Tribunal for the Former Yugoslavia (ICTY) (see Chapters 6 and 8) |
| 1994 | Russian combat troops sent to Chechnya to suppress secessionist attempt |
| 1994 | Rwandan genocide (see Chapter 6); UN creates International Criminal Tribunal for Rwanda (ICTR) (see Chapters 6 and 8) |
| 1998 | Statute for an International Criminal Court agreed in Rome |
| 1998 | First conviction for genocide at the ICTR |
| 1998–99 | Genocide in Kosovo (see Chapter 6) |
| 1999 | Genocide in East Timor (see Chapter 7) |
| 2001 | First conviction for genocide at the ICTY |
| 2002 | Slobodan Milosevic, former President of Serbia on trial for genocide, war crimes and crimes against humanity at the ICTY |
| 2002 | ICC comes into force; US signature to Rome Statute suspended by President Bush |
| 2003– | Genocide in Darfur (see Chapter 7) |
| 2009–10 | President Al-Bashir of Sudan indicted by the ICC for war crimes and crimes against humanity; subsequently also for genocide |

# Maps

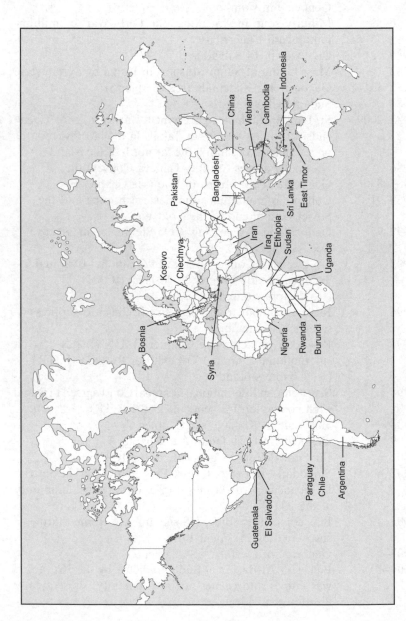

*Map 1*  Genocides and politicides since 1945

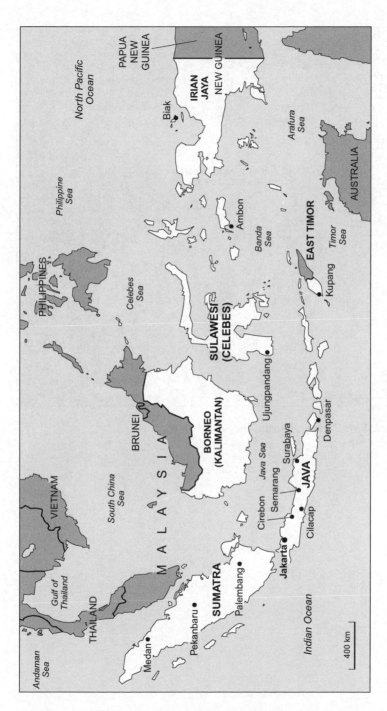

*Map 2* Indonesia and East Timor (see pp.57–61 and pp.99–100)

*Map 3* East Pakistan/Bangladesh (see pp.61–6)

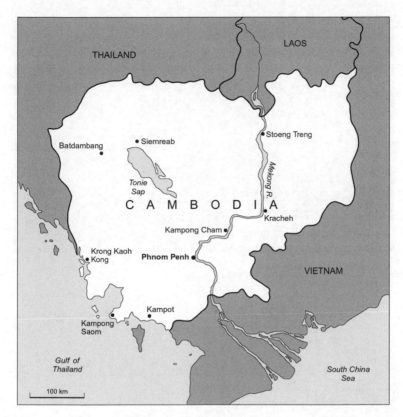

*Map 4* Cambodia (see pp.66–72)

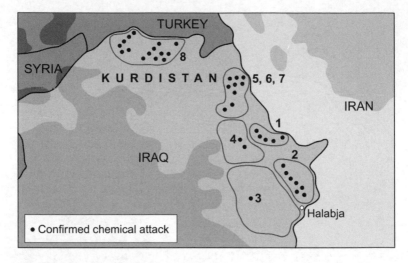

*Map 5* Iraq and Kurdistan (see pp.78–82)

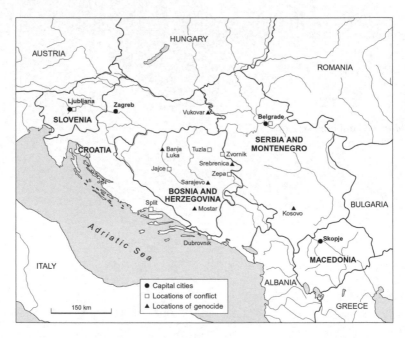

*Map 6* The former Yugoslavia (see pp.83–90)

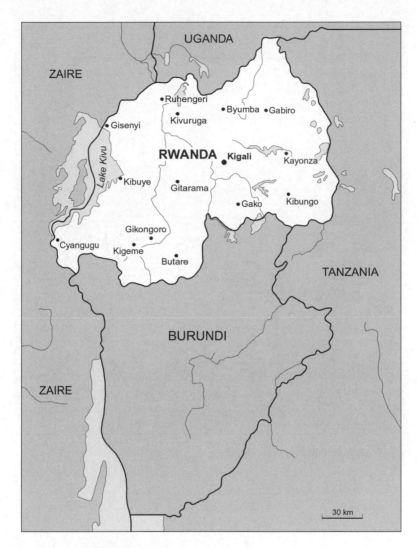

*Map 7* Rwanda (see pp.90–8)

*Map 8*  Map 8 Sudan (see pp.110–12)

# Introduction

It is now over 60 years since the United Nations passed the Genocide Convention. If there was one single idea behind the Convention, it was encapsulated in two words – 'Never Again', which expressed many people's reactions to the Holocaust. Rather than 'never again', however, it has sometimes since then seemed almost the opposite – not so much 'never again' as 'over and over again'. If genocide is not indeed central to the modern world (and there are powerful reasons for considering that it is), it certainly continues to disfigure it.

Reading and writing about genocide can at times, it must be confessed, be a disheartening experience. Some of what is described in these pages is hard to contemplate. It is tempting at times to want to put your head in your hands. I confess that I have done this on more than one occasion myself in the course of writing this book. But the questions that genocide poses are so fundamental that they keep demanding a response. Why do states, which are supposed to protect their citizens, turn on some of them and try to destroy them? Why do quite large numbers of people participate in the persecution, torture and murder of their fellow citizens, sometimes of those who had been their neighbours? Why do others (an even larger number) collaborate or watch while their fellow citizens are being eliminated? Why do some people come to their aid? What happens to victims and how can they respond? What responsibility do others have, beyond the borders of the state and society where genocide is occurring or threatening? What has the international community done to halt or prevent genocide, and what should it do? What should be done to bring the perpetrators of genocide to justice and what would justice look like? How can victims rebuild their lives?

These are difficult and challenging questions, not least because for many who write about genocide there is a necessary connection between scholarship and activism. On this, as on almost all other questions, there can be very different answers. This is perhaps particularly the case when it comes to questions of agency and responsibility, and of what action should or should not be taken to halt or prevent genocide; questions which form in some ways the central thread running through this book. Sometimes a consensus can be reached; at other times it cannot, at least for the moment. Some of these questions are resolvable; some are not, because there is no agreement sometimes about the very concepts we need to think about them. As I show in the course of this book, however, there is no escaping the reality that any research on genocide is always, in some degree, an act of engagement and responsibility. That is true of this volume, which draws on my research on genocide and the relationship between the Holocaust and subsequent genocides, and on my own related engagement with the Wiener Library as it has expanded its remit to become a resource for the study of both.

With a subject like genocide, disagreement and uncertainty is probably inevitable and may even be no bad thing. The challenge genocide poses to our understanding of the world we live in, the modern world, is profound and inherently unsettling. In a sense, our uncertainty may be taken as the opposite of the often terrifying certainty of those who decide upon genocide itself.

## Structure of the book

The crime of genocide was first identified by Raphael Lemkin. Chapter 1 looks at how and why Lemkin developed the concept of genocide and then traces the process through which the newly formed United Nations came to adopt the Convention. Despite the compromises that were involved and the failure of some states to ratify the Convention (notably the United States), it concludes that this was a truly historic development.

Chapter 2 looks at a number of issues raised by the Convention. It considers a number of objections to the way in which the Convention defines genocide, some of the apparent omissions, and some of the ways in which it might be strengthened. It highlights the failure to prosecute perpetrators and the recurrence of genocide, before considering whether the concept or the Convention needs to be abandoned or replaced.

Chapter 3 looks at a number of approaches that have been taken to explain why genocide takes place in the modern world. It begins by recognising the work of pioneers in the field, before going on to look at more recent arguments. Among the issues it discusses are the motives and ideologies of genocidal elites, the connections between genocide and war and revolution, or with colonialism and imperialism, and the extent to which genocide may be rooted in the international state system itself.

Chapter 4 looks at the question of participation and at the different roles of perpetrators, bystanders, victims and also rescuers in the genocidal process. It considers a variety of different approaches to this set of problems, and at a number of competing explanations, from a variety of disciplines.

At various points in the first four chapters, there are references forward to the case studies, which take up Chapters 5 and 6. Those readers anxious to acquaint themselves with details of what actually happened in these genocides can read forward at any point.

The first set of case studies in Chapter 5 are taken from the period of the Cold War, which made it very difficult to acknowledge, let alone halt genocides. The cases discussed here are the genocides in Indonesia, Bangladesh, Cambodia and Guatemala. In the following chapter, the cases looked at are the genocides which took place after the Cold War ended, in Iraq, the former Yugoslavia and Rwanda.

The failure in the last two cases to halt genocide triggered a major rethink about intervention, which is the focus of Chapter 7. This begins by noting the contrast between what happened in East Timor and the failures to intervene in Rwanda and Yugoslavia, before looking at the emergence of a new doctrine, the Responsibility to Protect. It then rehearses some of the key arguments about the desirability or otherwise of military intervention, before ending with a discussion of the failure to halt the more recent (but contested) case of genocide in Darfur.

Chapter 8 then looks at two sets of issues: one to do with what happens after genocide – the question of justice; the other with what can be done before genocide occurs – the question of prevention.

The book concludes with an assessment of the state of the politics of genocide today.

# 1 Never again? From the Holocaust to the Genocide Convention

## After the Holocaust

In January 1945, Soviet soldiers entered the extermination camp in Auschwitz in Poland, where over a million people, the overwhelming majority Jews, had been systematically murdered in the space of a few short years. Terrible as they were, Auschwitz and the extermination camps were 'only' one element in the Holocaust. A million had been shot before they were set up; many others had died already in ghettos and transportations; others died in death marches back to Germany as the Red Army advanced. Even as the Nazis faced certain defeat, priority had been given to murdering Jews over the war effort itself.

But Jews were not the Nazis' only victims. A large percentage of Sinti and Roma (around 200,000) were killed in what has become known as the *Porrajmos*; many millions of Poles, Russians, prisoners of war (3.3 million), thousands of disabled people, so-called 'social undesirables', and political opponents had also been murdered or starved to death.

This scale of destruction was more than the outcome of war, terrible though that had now become. After the horrors of the First World War, there had been considerable and anguished debate about what would happen if there was another war. But hardly anyone had predicted anything like the Holocaust.

## Raphael Lemkin

One of the few who had sensed something catastrophic was coming was a young Jewish lawyer from Poland. Raphael Lemkin had escaped himself to the United States but lost 49 members of his family in the Holocaust. Lemkin died in poverty and almost total obscurity but has now come to be recognised as one of the great moral figures of the twentieth century. As a young man, Lemkin had been shocked to discover that the organisers of the mass killing of Armenians during the First World War had not been prosecuted because there was no law under which they could be tried. What, Lemkin asked himself, was this crime that could not be punished? Was it new or old? Why was there no law against it and what could be done about it?

Lemkin's effort to answer these questions led him to develop a new concept: genocide. In the process, Lemkin drew on both his legal training and historical scholarship, and law and history have been intertwined in this question from the beginning, even if lawyers and historians have different objectives and concerns.

Lemkin's first effort was to think about the problem in terms of what he called 'barbarity' and 'vandalism', terms he proposed to a conference in Madrid in 1933. 'Barbarity' referred to 'acts of extermination'; 'vandalism' to attempts to destroy culture. Evocative though they were, these terms did not seem to quite capture the urgency of the problem in the contemporary world. The former in particular could be said to look back in some way, to take mankind back to a supposedly less civilised state. What Lemkin thought was taking place now, however, was not simply a regression.

In 1944 Lemkin produced an extensive study of what the Germans and their allies were doing in his book *Axis Rule in Occupied Europe*, paying detailed attention as a legal expert to laws and decrees, but also highlighting the Nazi state's more general imperialist and colonising plans for the East.[1] This was where he first deployed the concept of genocide to capture what he had come to see as a modern crime. What was modern was not mass murder, although the scale of it was now becoming immense. As Lemkin knew perfectly well, human beings have slaughtered each other for centuries. What was new was the way modern states were now trying to destroy groups entirely, or to cripple them to such an extent that they could not continue *as* recognisable groups. Mass killing was one (horrific) part of a wider problem, the destruction of groups, each of which made its own distinctive cultural contribution to the life of humanity. Lemkin believed that 'if the diversity of cultures were destroyed, it would be as disastrous for civilisation as the physical destruction of nations'.[2] Looking at what the Nazis were doing, Lemkin found evidence of what he called

> a co-ordinated plan of different actions aiming at ... the disintegra-
> tion of the political and social institutions, of culture, language,
> national feelings, religion, and the economic existence of national
> groups, and the destruction of the personal security, liberty, health,

dignity and even the lives of the individuals belonging to such groups.[3]

Lemkin was not always completely consistent in the way he used his new concept, perhaps not surprisingly, given the very difficult circumstances in which he was working, and the different audiences he was trying to address.[4] At times, he seemed to focus on extermination and mass killing, and physical violence was always central to his conception of genocide. But the main thrust was to emphasise the variety of methods used to attack 'different aspects of the life of the captive peoples' – the political, social, cultural, economic, biological, physical, religious and moral. At times too, he seemed to distinguish clearly between what happened to the Jews, with whom he closely identified and who the Nazis sought to annihilate immediately and physically entirely, and others who the Nazis also sought to destroy but not necessarily immediately, not necessarily totally and not necessarily through mass killing.[5] But again, the main thrust was to stress the connection, showing how all of the groups targeted by the Nazis were slated for destruction, sooner or later.

The target in any event in every case was less the individual *per se* than he or she as a member of a group. It was the group that was to be crippled, its 'essential foundations' destroyed so that it could be replaced by something else. For genocide, as Lemkin understood it, was a two-sided phenomenon, or one with two connected phases: 'one, the destruction of the national pattern of the oppressed group; the other, the imposition of the national pattern of the oppressor'.[6]

This result, moreover, could be achieved even if states were to lose a war. Even though Germany had in the end been defeated, the Nazis had succeeded in making much of Europe largely *Judenrein* – clear of Jews. Across Europe, over 70 per cent of the Jewish population was murdered and in some places the figures were even higher – 85 per cent in Poland, 89 per cent in Latvia and 90 per cent in Lithuania. Jews were brought from all over Europe to be killed – from Greece, for example (65,000 out of a total Jewish population of 75,000), or from Holland (90,000 from a pre-war community of some 150,000).[7]

The word that Lemkin invented, genocide, was a compound of words from the Greek (*genos* referring to a group) and Latin (from *caedere*, to kill). In drawing on the dead languages of the classical world, one could say that this term too still looked back. But the creation of this new word nevertheless struck a chord with others.

Already in 1941, in denouncing the atrocities of the Nazis, Churchill had claimed that 'we are in the presence of a crime without a name'.[8]

This did not mean that Churchill or other Allied leaders were entirely clear with their publics about what was happening. In fact they largely downplayed what the Nazis were doing to the Jews, not because of a lack of information but because it was not a strategic or moral priority.[9] Their states had not gone to war with Nazi Germany to save the Jews and they saw no value in giving the erroneous impression that they were now fighting for this reason. Even after the war, what happened to Jews was still not highlighted in films, reports and broadcasts.[10]

## Nuremburg, crimes of war and genocide

This was true even in the historic trial of leading Nazis which took place at Nuremburg in 1946, where the focus was not primarily on the murder of Jews, but on crimes of war and aggression.[11] This seriously limited the extent to which genocide could feature as an issue.

The Allies had been divided initially on what they should do with the Nazi leaders. In the end, the Allies decided to hold a trial but there was considerable uncertainty about who exactly should be arraigned and on what charges. A central problem had to do with the question of national sovereignty. As Justice Robert Jackson put it at the London Conference that paved the way for Nuremburg,

> the way Germany treats its inhabitants, or any other country treats its inhabitants is not our affair any more than it is the affair of some other government to interpose itself into our problems. The reason that this program of exterminating the Jews ... becomes an international concern is this: it was a part of a plan for making an illegal war. Unless we have a war connection as a basis for reaching them ... we have no basis for dealing with atrocities.[12]

This overriding emphasis on war was a significant impediment to thinking more clearly about genocide in another important sense. The notion of war crimes had after all already been established in the Hague Conventions of 1899 and 1907 and in the Geneva Protocol of 1925. If the Nazis could be prosecuted for the crime of waging an aggressive war within which they had committed mass murder and other atrocities, why was a new concept or law necessary? The problem was that the Nazis had clearly committed them *before* the war, as well as during it. The prosecutors at Nuremburg tried to get round this problem by charging the Nazis with *conspiracy* to wage aggressive war but this was clearly not very satisfactory.

The term genocide was in fact invoked on several occasions, sometimes with specific reference to Lemkin himself. It featured for example both in the indictment and in the prosecutor's closing arguments. It did not appear, however, in either the final judgement or in the Charter of the International Military Tribunal itself.

Lemkin was dismayed by this conclusion, as he had intended his new concept to cover crimes committed not only in times of war but also in peace. But he did not give up, and others in any case were already beginning to use the term more freely. Alongside Nuremburg, other trials of Nazi criminals were also taking place, in Poland and in occupied Germany, where the term genocide began to appear more and more.

## Drafting the Convention[13]

Immediately after the Nuremburg Trial verdicts had been handed down in late 1946, discussion continued at the first United Nations General Assembly. On 11 December 1946, the General Assembly passed unanimously Resolution 96(I), which asserted the gravity of genocide and the threat it posed to humanity itself. Genocide was defined as

> a denial of the right of existence of entire human groups, as homicide is the denial of the right to live of individual human beings; such denial of the right of existence shocks the conscience of mankind, resulting in great losses to humanity in the form of cultural and other contributions represented by these human groups, and is contrary to the moral law and to the spirit and aims of the United Nations.

The Resolution identified genocide as 'a crime under international law' and called on Member States both to 'enact the necessary legislation for the prevention and punishment of the crime' and to 'co-operate speedily to prevent and punish it'. The Assembly then mandated its Economic and Social Council to draft a Convention on genocide for its next session.

This was a momentous move. Although the General Assembly is not a law-making body, it had now called for commitments which went significantly beyond what had previously been agreed between states in any international forum or organisation.

The radical character of this declaration and the call for a Convention troubled some participants. The Economic and Social Council was not able to make a great deal of progress as a result and the matter then came back to the Assembly for its second session from September to December 1947 which handed the drafting over to its 6th (Legal) Committee. Here too there was considerable debate and the 6th Committee appeared rather to water down the spirit of the original Declaration, even to the point of suggesting a Convention might not be desirable or necessary at all. Many in the General Assembly were irritated by this. Resolution 180(II) reaffirmed the urgent need for a Convention, along the lines originally expressed. An *ad hoc* committee of the Economic and Social Council was formed to speed up the drafting. Finally, after considerably more debate (at no less than 28 meetings), the Assembly adopted Resolution 260(III) A on 9 December 1948 (some 24 hours before the Universal Declaration on Human Rights), as the Convention on the Prevention and Punishment of the Crime of Genocide (see Appendix 1).

### Ratifying the Convention

Lemkin's work, however, was not finished. The Convention still needed to be ratified by at least 20 states. Ethiopia was the first to do so and, by 11 December, 42 other states had also done so. The Convention itself came into force on 12 January 1951.

One state however refused to ratify it – the United States. This came as a great shock to Lemkin, who was to spend several more years fruitlessly attempting to have this decision changed. Although the United States had taken a leading role at Nuremburg and been engaged throughout the drafting process, strong opposition to the Convention emerged in Congress. This was largely on grounds of sovereignty, with critics fearing that the Convention would be used against the United States for what it might do or had done in the past, even though the Convention was not retroactive.

This was a serious blow to Lemkin but also foreshadowed critical problems with the Convention in the future, which hinge in many ways on the problem of the sovereignty of the nation state, as we shall see. Lemkin died long before the United States changed its position. It was to do so only in the 1980s. When the decision was made, it was not exactly the result of a major rethink but to appease those outraged by President Reagan when he visited an SS war memorial at Bitburg in Germany.

The United States of course was not the only state not to ratify the Convention. To date not all member states of the United Nations (UN) have signed up, although the large majority (140) have done so.

Even if later than Lemkin would have wished, the Convention does command adherence from a large majority of states, including the most powerful.

## The significance of the Convention

For all the subsequent difficulties, many of which will be rehearsed in the rest of this book, this was a remarkable achievement. A new concept had been forged to express a new understanding of what could happen in the modern world. A grave crime had been identified, what would in a later Tribunal be called the 'crime of crimes'.[14]

This is not to say that the Convention is a sufficient response to the problem, even on paper. Identifying a crime does not by itself make the crime disappear and genocide has certainly not done so. Nor was the identification of the crime itself perfect. As the debates in the drafting process had already showed, there were several issues which were highly contestable and have continued to haunt the question of genocide ever since.

This is hardly surprising. The issues that the Convention raised were not only legal. They were also inherently political and ethical. In this forum, the newly associated member states were being confronted with questions that related not just to what Nazi Germany had just done. They raised questions too about moral standards, about what human beings are capable of and about what humanity itself should and should not permit, even about what humanity itself is at some level. To attempt to eliminate a group is, after all, to seek to change the composition of humanity itself.

For all its difficulties, several of which are discussed in the next chapter, the Convention nevertheless does do much to capture the gravity of the threat posed by genocide. It does more than identify it as 'a crime under international law'. It is something which has to be 'condemned by the civilized world'; it is 'an odious scourge, from which mankind must be liberated'.

These are not idle words. The drafters of the Convention clearly felt that genocide was a matter of supreme importance which had to be addressed by the newly formed international community from the outset. In that sense, there is perhaps something symbolic in the fact that it was passed 24 hours before the Universal Declaration of Human Rights, although it is clearly connected to it in many ways. Like Lemkin, they saw genocide as a fundamental challenge to which humanity itself had to respond. Were they right to do so?

Again, we need to go back to the Holocaust and to Lemkin's sense that something new was taking place. A conscious effort had just been made to eliminate a group entirely from the earth. As Hannah Arendt (to whom we shall return) put it, the Holocaust was 'the supreme crime' not just because of what was done to the Jews but, even more fundamentally, because 'genocide ... is an attack upon human diversity as such'.[15]

Arendt argued that the problem posed by the Nazis was that what they had almost succeeded in doing could become a precedent for others to follow.

> It is in the very nature of things human that every act that has once made its appearance and has been recorded in the history of mankind stays with mankind as potentiality ... if genocide is an actual possibility of the future, then no people on earth – least of all, of course, the Jewish people, in Israel or elsewhere – can feel reasonably sure of its continued existence without the help and protection of international law.[16]

In many ways, that protection was what Lemkin and the Convention sought to provide. How well that protection has in fact been provided (or indeed can be) is something we discuss in the rest of this book.

# 2 The Genocide Convention

The Genocide Convention contains some 19 articles. The first nine of these are the most important (see Appendix 1) and especially:

- Article II, where the crime of genocide is defined
- Article III, which lists the punishable acts
- Article IV, which identifies who can be punished
- Articles V and VIII, which impose responsibilities on or call for action from the Contracting Parties
- Article VI which calls for the setting-up of tribunals.

None of these are straightforward. Ever since the Convention was first mooted, there has been continued debate about several key issues. In particular:

- Are all acts of genocide of equivalent gravity?
- How many people have to be killed for something to count as genocide?
- Does genocide have to involve the destruction of the whole group?
- Is there a distinction between the destruction and the wholesale removal of a group?
- What exactly is genocidal intent and how can it be proved?
- Why were only certain groups identified for protection?
- Who are the most likely perpetrators?
- Where and how can perpetrators be prosecuted?

## Acts of genocide – from killing to cultural destruction?

The Convention of course was by no means all Lemkin's work. As used in the Convention, genocide had a narrower meaning than the one he had originally proposed. It conveys less sense of a co-ordinated attack and there is no explicit reference in particular to the question of cultural destruction.[1] Lemkin himself was dismayed by this omission, as he was particularly concerned with this dimension to genocide, as we have seen.

The idea that the destruction of culture could be put on a par with mass killing, however, had been sharply criticised in the drafting process, where the Danish delegate had argued that closing libraries could simply not be equated with mass murder. If the idea remains, it is largely to be found in the last of the acts listed in Article II – 'forcibly transferring children of the group to another group'. This was only included however with the qualifier 'forcibly', in order to reaffirm the emphasis on physical destruction.[2] Even so, is it right to equate it with killing?

Transferring children from one group to another might actually mean in some circumstances, for example, an improved standard of living, even of life expectancy. On the other hand, the grave concern expressed here is not to do with life as such so much as with identity, with how life can be lived, in what ways and according to whose values, beliefs and norms. This is perhaps even more of a concern today. Many now argue that cultural identity is core to who people are, to how they think and feel about themselves. To have one's identity taken away and to be forced to adopt another is seen as a fundamental violation of the person, as well as attacking the cultural diversity of humanity.

Whether it is quite the same as killing is, however, not so clear. It could be argued that killing is not only rightly at the top of the list but that it is quite different to the other acts named, at least to (d) (preventing births within the group) and (e) (transferring children). Imposing conditions calculated to bring about destruction seems extremely close, and serious harm clearly involves suffering that could make life itself unbearable. But killing is direct and immediate. It means ceasing to exist at all, whatever the importance of culture or identity.

## Numbers – in whole or in part?

This is sometimes taken further. Genocide, it is often thought, means not just the loss of one life but of many lives. It is not just individual murder but mass murder. In fact, the Convention does not make this leap. Even if killing is at the top of the list, it does not have to take place in any large number for genocide to be charged. There is no reference in the text to number at all. In principle, the number killed could be as low as one. This would be a very peculiar reading, given that the preamble speaks of acts committed with intent to destroy, in whole or in part. This has given rise to considerable argument, since it is not clear what is meant by 'in part'.

One way of thinking about this is to distinguish between quantitative and qualitative aspects of the process of destruction.[3] The latter might involve the targeting of particular groups within the overall group, without whose leadership the group might find it hard to survive. Perpetrators of genocide indeed often seem to have such a 'decapitation' tactic in mind. Or it might involve an attack on a group in a particular geographical area which lies at the heart of the group's existence. Without a political or cultural or physical core, the group would find it difficult to sustain itself, to retain sufficient cohesion or sense of purpose.

## Genocide and ethnic cleansing

One problem with such a 'geographical' understanding of genocide, however, is that it raises questions about the difference between removing a group from a particular place and destroying it as such. In recent years, a new term has emerged, 'ethnic cleansing', which might be distinguished from genocide, although some think it is simply a euphemism.[4] It is true that forcing people out of a place to which they feel profoundly attached as their home on earth is not easy to distinguish from genocide. The force required to compel a group to move is likely to involve similar kinds of acts to those enumerated in Article II. It can include mass killing, and the use of terror against unarmed civilians, as well as starvation and disease. If the aim is to remove people permanently from an area, it is likely to involve efforts to remove all traces of their having lived there and, through the use of mass rape especially, making it impossible for the community to reproduce itself in that space.[5]

There are, however, some possible differences. Ethnic cleansing involves a contest (however unequal) between rival groups contending for the same area, even though civilians are the central target. The motive appears to be essentially to do with territory which may in fact be exchanged, a possibility not mentioned in the Convention. Genocides though are not only about territory. Even if ethnic cleansing clearly involves extensive destruction, it is possible for people to flee and reconstitute their group somewhere else. From the ethnic cleansers' point of view, as long as the group is gone from that area, they may not need to destroy it.

Rather than thinking about ethnic cleansing as coterminous with genocide, it perhaps makes more sense to see it as overlapping.[6] Ethnic cleansing shares certain features with genocide. Any case of ethnic conflict, particularly where there is inequality in power between the rival groups, is bound to raise concerns about the possibility of genocide. Ethnic cleansing can become genocide, perhaps quite quickly, but it does not start out or always end up as the same thing.

## Intent

Part of the problem here arises from trying to establish what purposes lie behind any of the acts committed. Genocide involves both a physical element (what is known in criminal law as the *actus reus*) and a mental element (the *mens rea*). The acts specified have to be undertaken with the *intent* to destroy the group. In some ways this is as important as the acts themselves. Indeed it is perfectly possible for there to be the intent to kill large numbers of people but for only one or a handful of people to be actually killed. The charge of genocide would still apply.

The term 'intent' did not actually appear in an earlier draft by the UN Secretariat at all but ended up playing a prominent role in the final text. It appears before any of the acts are listed which define genocide itself. There is a reason for this. From a legal point of view, intent is what sets criminal law apart.[7] An important part of what makes an offence criminal is the state of mind of the person committing the act. He or she has to know what they are doing. But this is not an easy thing to determine, even in domestic penal law. Intent may make sense when thinking about persons, who have minds of their own. But do groups, and especially states, have minds of their own in the same sense?

Perhaps a more serious problem still is quite what is meant by intent in the first place. The first paragraph or chapeau of Article II defines it as intent 'to destroy in whole or in part a ... group as such'. It is often assumed therefore that intent has to be specific or special, what is known as *dolus specialis*. Many experts argue that this is what distinguishes genocide from other crimes, and that the specific intent has to be proven for the charge of genocide to stand.[8] A more flexible, looser interpretation would be to think in terms of knowledge, that the act or acts are committed by the perpetrator knowing that they will or are likely to destroy the group.[9] Legal commentators and the courts appear to have been torn between these two approaches – the one purpose-based, the other knowledge-based. The International Court of Justice adopted the former but the Rwanda Tribunal used the latter, arguing that a perpetrator 'is culpable because he or she knew or should have known that the act committed would destroy, in whole or in part, a group'.[10]

The question of intent is one where there may be a particular tension between law and history. Many historians prefer to think more in terms of structures rather than intent (see Chapter 3), not least because it can be difficult to establish a clear and direct link between a state of mind at one point in time and an action much later. Motives can be complex and change over time and often can be difficult to ascertain with any certainty.

On the other hand, it is important to distinguish between specific *intent* and *motive*. This indeed is what the courts have done, finding (as one judgement has put it) that

> the personal motive of the perpetrator of the crime of genocide may be, for example, to obtain personal economic benefits, or political advantage, or some form of power. The existence of a personal motive does not preclude the perpetrator from also having the specific intent to commit genocide.[11]

## Intent or outcome?

Rather than going down the problematic path of trying to ascertain and prove intent, it might be better to look at outcomes. Genocide may not be intended, but the outcomes of certain actions may be very likely to be genocidal. It may not be necessary to have a coherent, articulated plan or policy at the outset. Both the first two kinds of acts (killing and causing serious bodily or mental harm) can clearly be committed without a worked-out plan for genocide. This is less likely perhaps with regard to the other acts, which seem to require some degree of prior planning.

The absence of a fully worked-out plan from the outset does not, however, imply innocence. On the contrary, it can be argued that intent can be inferred from the actions taken, in a sense reversing the order of presentation in the Convention – from act *to* intent. Critical court judgements in recent years seem to have gone in this direction, precisely because it has been difficult otherwise to prove intent. The organisers of genocide have usually been clever enough not to leave evidence if they could avoid it. Hitler famously did not issue a written order instructing his subordinates to organise the extermination of the Jews. Holocaust deniers have used this to claim that he knew nothing about what happened or indeed that there could not have been a Holocaust at all. In order to avoid falling into this trap, courts have found that genocide can be inferred: from the general context; from other acts of a grave kind that were taking place; from the scale of atrocities; from the systematic targeting of particular groups; and from the repetition of destructive acts carried against them.[12]

On the other hand, this might lead to the assumption that genocide has to take place for the charge to be proven. But this is not actually what the Convention stipulates. Genocide can be intended even if it does not in the end take place. Plans for genocide can fail or be abandoned. It is not difficult to see how this could cause further difficulties. It can be hard enough to prove that there was prior intent when genocide has taken place. It is even harder to prove there was intent when genocide did not occur.

## Groups

Whilst all of these have proved to be thorny problems, there are still others, especially relating to the question of groups. There are four groups of potential victims identified in the Convention – 'national, ethnical, racial and religious'. The obvious question is why these? Lemkin did not use all of these categories in his definition in 1944, where he focused on the national group. This category alone is problematic enough, as there are a number of competing conceptions of what constitutes a nation. One answer is that a nation is based on an ethnic 'core', in which case it is not entirely obvious why we need a different category of 'ethnical' (sic).

Alternatively, it might be argued that ethnicity is not that different to race, and there was quite a lot of debate about this at the 6th Committee. On the other hand, the idea of race had been discredited by Nazism to some extent (at least as a biological category),[13] and of course has no scientific validity at all. One can talk of *racialised* groups, groups which are said by racists to be races, but that is rather different, since it points precisely to the way in which race is used (by racists) to define people for negative and demeaning purposes.

What this suggests is that it might be better to think about these groups as existing in the eye of the perpetrator, and not, as was widely believed in 1948, because they were real, existing entities. This more nuanced understanding was first proposed by Frank Chalk and Kurt Jonassohn[14] and their approach has been endorsed by recent tribunals and courts. Rather than becoming bogged down in debates about the objectivity or otherwise of groups, they have concluded (in the words of one important judgement) that 'it is more appropriate to evaluate the status of a national, ethnical or racial group from the point of view of those persons who wish to single out that group from the rest of the community'.[15]

There remains, however, the question of why only these groups were chosen. One answer might be that they just are the most important, that nationality, or ethnicity or religion (if no longer race) really are the most important ways in which people identify themselves or are identified.[16] One could also argue that these overlap quite often, so reinforcing their significance, or that even if one group definition does not work, another one of these makes sense. Not all Jews for example might be included under the category of religion but could perhaps be in terms of ethnicity. Many Jews who were swept up in the Holocaust were clearly not religious in any way.

## Political and social groups

But this still leaves at least one crucial question unanswered. Why were political and social groups not included in the list? For many people, this is the most serious omission in the Convention. One reason for this concern is that political and social groups have so often been the target. This was clearly the case for the Soviet Union under Stalin, when huge numbers of people were murdered by the state. Whilst some of these victims could be categorised in ethnic or national terms – Ukrainians in the early 1930s or Chechens, Ingush and Crimean Tatars in the 1940s, for example – many were clearly killed as 'enemies of the people', as they were in Cambodia later.

There was in fact considerable debate about this issue from the very beginning. Political and social groups were referred to both in Resolution 96(I) and in the first draft. The major state to object was, not surprisingly, the Soviet Union. Its delegate claimed that genocide was 'organically bound up with Nazism-Fascism and other similar race "theories" which preach racial or national hatred, the domination of so-called "higher" races and the extermination of so-called "lower" races'.[17] But the Soviet Union was not alone. Poland objected too, on the grounds that political groups were not permanent or stable, whilst Venezuela feared that political groups would abuse the Convention. Raphael Lemkin himself was also against the inclusion of political groups, partly because of his deep concern with culture, partly for the same reason as the Polish delegate and partly because he feared that 'the Convention should not run the risk of failure by introducing ideas on which the world is so divided'.[18]

These objections point to real and continuing problems. It can be argued that political groups, unlike national or ethnic ones, are freely chosen. People are born into nations or ethnic groups, whilst political affiliation is a matter of choice. One can abandon one's political commitments in a way one cannot perhaps renounce a national or ethnic identity. This distinction is less compelling in the case of religion, but here the overlapping argument can be used to counter this objection, inasmuch as religious affiliation is often tied up with national or ethnic identity.

So too, however, it can be argued, is politics. Moreover, there is a grave danger that states can use the exclusion of political groups to redescribe what they are doing so that it no longer appears to be genocide at all. They can use it as a 'get-out' clause, as it were, arguing that their victims are not members of a national, ethnic or religious group but constitute a political threat to the state against which it has the right to defend itself.[19]

Several genocide scholars have argued (quite persuasively in my view) that the exclusion of political groups was a critical weakness in the Convention. In the words of one, 'the exclusion of political groups ... insulates political leaders from being charged with the very crime they may be most likely to commit: the extermination of politically threatening groups'.[20]

One answer, offered by Barbara Harff and Ted Gurr, was that there should be an additional term to cover the destruction of political groups, what they have called 'politicide'.[21] Another answer, of course, is to amend the Convention. The difficulty is that the UN has proven very resistant to any effort to change the Convention. In 1985, for example, Benjamin Whitaker produced a report for the UN on how the Convention had fared, which called for a broader definition.[22] The controversy this produced meant that his report could not even be tabled.

The question of groups remains an inherently contested one. Like many other writers on the subject, I have found the exclusion of political groups unpersuasive and dangerously limiting. A number of cases discussed in this book include efforts by states to destroy them (although not only them). Readers may judge for themselves how convincing it is to include these as cases of genocide.

## States

The argument that states are only defending themselves against an internal threat effectively reverses one important thrust of the Convention which has to do with conspiracy (see Article III[b]). But the problem that the Convention was trying to deal with could in some ways be thought about as rather the opposite – a conspiracy by a state against groups of people, not by groups of people against the state. This was precisely Lemkin's starting-point – that in the modern world it is states which have the power and capacity to organise and plan the destruction of groups, not the other way round.

The Convention does not, however, identify states clearly as potential perpetrators. Articles II and III refer to acts which may be committed and should be punished; Articles IV, V and VI refer to 'persons' who shall be punished or for whom effective penalties should be provided or who should be charged and tried. Article IX does talk of 'the responsibility of a State for genocide' but, as John Quigley has argued, this term sits uneasily with the term 'punishable' which is aimed at individuals, and it might have been better to use the term 'liable' rather than 'responsible'.[23]

This ambiguity was probably not an accident. There was considerable debate about the question of state responsibility in the drafting process. The United Kingdom tried hard to insert the concept of state responsibility into the Convention but was opposed, particularly by France but also by the two superpowers, although in the end it lost only very narrowly (by just two votes).

France was keen to keep the focus on individual responsibility and it is of course right to remember that individuals commit crimes. This was a point made forcefully and famously by the Nuremberg Tribunal when it stated that 'crimes against international law are committed by men, not by abstract entities'.[24] But this was to reject the defence that individuals were only following orders. It should not be taken to mean that the state itself did not have a fundamental responsibility for organising genocide.

The absence of a central, direct and explicit reference to states as perpetrators was a major problem for some time. It can be argued that in an earlier period and in many cases of genocides connected to settler-colonialism (see Chapter 3), the state's role had more of an effectively permissive and enabling character, allowing genocide to take place and then consistently sanctioning it (to its own advantage). But increasingly and certainly since 1945, the state has clearly played more of an organising and directing role. It is difficult to see how this could be otherwise. If, as Lemkin believed, genocide requires a sustained and co-ordinated attack on a group on several fronts, only a modern state has (to date) had the capacity to mount one. As William Schabas has argued, 'while exceptions cannot be ruled out, it is virtually impossible to imagine genocide that is not planned and organised either by the state itself or by some clique associated with it'.[25]

The responsibility of the state has gradually been recognised, and again courts have played an important role in clarifying the issue. In 1996, the International Court of Justice (ICJ) decided that states could indeed be sued for perpetrating genocide under the Convention. However, it then found that Serbia (which was being sued by Bosnia) was not itself the perpetrator but was guilty only of the failure to punish and prevent, much to the dismay of many of the victims (see Chapter 6). This was partly the result of the Court setting the threshold very high, using the narrow reading of special intent (see above).[26]

Leaving aside the peculiarities of the reasoning of the ICJ in this particular case, there may be deeper reasons why it was difficult for so long to focus directly on the central role of states in genocide. Even as the members of the UN were trying to address the question of genocide, they might have been uncomfortably aware that the charge might come to be laid against them, and not only for what they might do in the future. Few states could look back with much confidence at their own history and not think that, at some stage or other, they had committed some or all of these acts themselves (see Chapter 3).

## Prosecution

Prosecution even of individuals has certainly been difficult. It took a very long time indeed before any progress was made with regard to Article VI, which proposes that, in the first instance, 'persons charged with genocide ... shall be tried by a competent tribunal of the State in the territory of which the act was committed'. This was bound to be highly unlikely from the first, unless there was a change of regime, as leaders of states would obviously not prosecute themselves. On the other hand, even if there is a change of regime, the chances of a fair trial could be quite remote. A new regime could include former members of the old regime who would be anxious to hide their own participation in the crime. Alternatively, if there has been a radical break, a new regime might seek revenge, implementing a victor's justice.

This was of course an accusation laid even against the Nuremburg Trials, which provided the precedent for the alternative in the second proposal in Article VI for an 'international penal tribunal'. No progress at all, however, was made for a very long time on this issue, until the setting up of *ad hoc* international tribunals to deal with the genocides in Yugoslavia and Rwanda (see Chapters 6 and 8). Only after they had paved the way was a permanent court set up to deal with genocide, the International Criminal Court (ICC) (see Chapter 8).

An international court, however, is not the only one which could prosecute for genocide. National courts outside the state where genocide took place could also do this, under the principle of universal jurisdiction, on the basis that genocide is a crime against mankind itself. Again though, it took a long time before this was considered. Universal jurisdiction was not recognised in the Convention but has subsequently been so in customary international law.[27] National courts have recently begun to move in this direction, with the case launched in Spain in 2008 against perpetrators of the genocide in Guatemala (see Chapter 5).

## The recurrence of genocide

It is too early to tell whether this will establish a secure precedent that others will act on. The harsh reality is that for a very long time after 1948 perpetrators of genocide went unpunished. The even harsher reality is that since the Convention was passed, there have been an alarmingly large number of genocides (see Table 2.1). There have been

*Table 2.1* Cases of genocide since 1948

| Location | Victims | (Approximate) numbers |
| --- | --- | --- |
| Rwanda 1963–4 | Tutsis | 12,000–20,000 |
| Burundi 1965–73 | Hutus | c.140,000 |
| Indonesia 1965–6 | 'Communists' | 500,000–1,000,000 |
| Nigeria (Biafra) 1966 | Ibos | c.1,000,000 |
| East Pakistan 1971 | Bengalis (Hindu and Muslim) | 1,000,000–3,000,000 |
| Paraguay 1974 | Guayaki Ache Indians | c.900,000 |
| Cambodia 1975–9 | Cambodians | 1,900,000–3,500,000 |
| East Timor 1975–99 | East Timorese | c.200,000 |
| Guatemala 1978–96 | Mayans and Leftists | c.250,000 |
| Sudan 1983– | Dinka, Nuer, Nuba, Fur, Zaghawa and Masalit | c.2,000,000 |
| Iraq 1988–91 | Kurds | c.180,000 |
| Burundi 1988 | Hutus | 5,000–20,000 |
| Iraq 1992 | Marsh Arabs | Unknown |
| Bosnia 1992–5 | Muslims | c.225,000 |
| Burundi 1993–4 | Hutus | c.50,000 |
| Rwanda 1994 | Tutsis and moderate Hutus | 500,000–1,000,000 |
| Chechnya 1994–2000 | Chechens | c.30,000 |
| Kosovo 1988–9 | Albanians | c.10,000 |
| Sri Lanka 2009 | Tamils | c.20,000 |

so many cases in fact that it could even be argued that there have been more genocides since the Convention than there were before. As Christopher Powell has pointed out, 'the era in which genocide was made criminal for the first time is also the era in which it achieved effects of scale, efficiency and frequency that stun the imagination'.[28]

Although this is an extensive enough list, especially with the addition of Harff's 'politicides', it is not definitive. Any list of genocides is likely to provoke charged debates about why some cases are included and others not. One of the reasons for this is that survivors of atrocities can fear that not affixing the label 'genocide' to what happened to their communities somehow relegates its significance, and makes it appear not so serious after all. This is often not an unreasonable fear. There is, sadly, more than enough evidence of people abusing semantic arguments about definition for malign purposes, even in the most clear-cut cases. As we shall see later, denial is an important last stage in the genocidal process (although not confined to it), further wounding the victimised group.[30]

Not all arguments of course are ill-intentioned. There is clearly scope for genuine disagreement about how broadly or narrowly genocide should be defined, provided it does not become mired in what William Schabas calls a 'definitional trap'.[31] Those who prefer a broad definition will want the term to embrace more than mass killing, to include cases where cultural destruction in particular was the outcome, and to include social and political groups in its compass. Conversely, those who prefer a narrow definition will be concerned with the number of deaths, want to see clear evidence of intent and to keep to the groups specified. My own view, as will be seen in the case studies, is that a broader definition is more helpful, but with mass killing kept at the core.

One apparent corollary of this debate is, however, worth dispelling before we go much further. It might be thought, on the face of it, that a narrow definition would guard against too sweeping an application of the Convention in terms of what Article VIII requires: that where genocide is recognised as taking place or to be threatening, the international community is obligated to intervene. In fact this obligation, as we shall see, has been very largely evaded. There have been hardly any interventions to halt genocide and those very few that have taken place have sparked intense debates about the legitimacy or wisdom of such actions (see Chapter 7).

But if this is the case, and if even a narrow reading of the Convention has not led either to the prevention of genocide or to its suppression, or (for a long time) to bringing perpetrators to justice, then some rather troubling questions arise. Is the Convention useless? Do we need something else? Or can nothing be done to bring an end to this 'odious scourge' (whatever it is)?

## Discarding or building on the Convention?

One view could certainly be that the concept of genocide itself should be discarded, as Christian Gerlach for example has argued. He thinks it is fatally flawed because there is no agreed definition; because it focuses on one group, when several are involved; because it concentrates too much on the state; because it excludes many kinds of violence; and because it looks in vain for intent when the real question is process. Above all, it encourages the belief that there are easy answers to complex problems. Instead of genocide, it would be much more helpful to think about mass violence, a term also favoured by Jacques Sémelin.[32] Gerlach advocates instead the notion of what he calls 'extremely violent societies'. Mass violence then has to be seen as a process in which several groups participate, not just the state, for varied reasons, and violence is frequently not targeted at just one group.[33]

Others would want to defend both the concept and the Convention. Critics of Gerlach have argued that his approach not only effectively erases genocidal agency but also ignores the long-term consequences of structures that have led to the elimination of many indigenous peoples. The concept of genocide, however slippery, captures both intent and outcome, planning and execution. Above all, it identifies a threat to humanity on an existential scale.[34]

## Genocide and crimes against humanity

This is not to deny that there are flaws in the Convention. However, some of these have been addressed in judgements made by the Tribunals and the ICC. As we have seen throughout this chapter, the International Criminal Tribunals for the former Yugoslavia and Rwanda (ICTY, the ICTR and the ICC) have developed the jurisprudence of genocide constructively in several areas, generally by interpreting the Convention more loosely. They have determined that: intent can be inferred; states do have responsibility not just for preventing genocide but can be seen as perpetrators; perpetrators can be convicted if they could have reasonably foreseen that the consequences of their actions were likely to be genocidal; rape is an important dimension of more than one set of genocidal acts; and recognised that cultural destruction (as Lemkin believed) is intimately connected to physical violence.[35]

A particularly important development, which may help to resolve some of the tensions around defining cases of genocide, as William Schabas in particular has argued, has been the way in which the notion of crimes against humanity has been expanded.[36] Although these were always close and overlapping in certain respects, there were originally at least three differences between crimes against humanity and genocide. The first was that crimes against humanity were seen primarily in the context of aggressive war, whereas genocide was defined as a crime that could be committed in times of war and peace. The second was that crimes against humanity were limited to attacks on civilian groups, whereas genocide is a crime that can also be committed against military groups. The third was that only genocide involves the intent to destroy a group. But the advent of the ICC, whose remit includes both crimes against humanity and genocide, as well as war crimes, has brought all of these more closely together.

## Genocide and atrocity crimes

That does not mean, of course, that there is not further work to be done. David Scheffer in particular has argued for a new unifying concept, that of 'atrocity crimes', to cover genocide, crimes of war and aggression, crimes against humanity and ethnic cleansing – all crimes that the ICC is charged with prosecuting.[37] Scheffer argues that this new umbrella concept is needed for both legal and political reasons.

From a legal point of view, this new terminology would capture a 'basket of particularly heinous crimes', committed on a major scale with a clearly destructive character. They all shock the conscience of mankind. From the political point of view, this would remove some of the obstacles behind which states can hide as they fail to halt or prevent genocide. Instead of becoming mired in problems which derive from the criminal context of the Convention, states would need to understand that responding to genocide is a political question. It is about taking responsibility in the face of impending catastrophe facing groups at the hands of perpetrators, typically leaders of other states. Instead of obsessing about intent or the precise nature of the likely crime, states need to act swiftly on a more 'liberal' understanding of genocide to prevent it happening, as soon as it threatens.

Scheffer's proposal is a bold attempt to build on the Convention and, even if not accepted by everyone, surely points us in the right direction. It acknowledges the real difficulties with the Convention but attempts to surmount them, linking genocide to other grave crimes without diminishing its significance. He also takes us back to the spirit of the reaction to the Holocaust that led to the Convention in the first place. Faced with the horrors of the Jewish genocide, there was a widely felt sense that something like this should never be allowed to happen again. For all the subsequent difficulties in defining what this was exactly, this was surely the right response. The Convention was grounded in the recognition that after the Holocaust humanity itself faced a profound legal, political and ethical challenge.

This challenge has not gone away. The fact that genocide has recurred despite the Convention is deeply troubling but should only redouble the need to understand why and how this has been the case.

# 3    Explaining genocide

Despite its recurrence, it took some time before the question of genocide attracted much attention. It was not really until after Holocaust studies had been firmly established that sustained research began into the subject. There is some debate, however, as to whether studying genocide in the shadow of the Holocaust has always been that helpful, even though without it there would have been no Genocide Convention and perhaps no concept of genocide itself. It has been argued that there is a danger in seeing the Holocaust as an 'ideal type' or placing it at the top of some kind of hierarchy.[1] On the other hand, the Holocaust has generated a very substantial literature (although there was in fact a significant time lag of some 15–20 years before this could happen)[2] which can be used to illuminate our understanding of genocide more generally.

In any event, there is now a substantial and growing body of work attempting to explain genocide. It draws on a range of disciplines, including history, political science, sociology, anthropology and psychology. It has not yet produced, and is perhaps unlikely to produce, any one overarching answer to the question of why genocides keep happening, not least because, as we shall see later from a number of cases, there are significant differences as well as similarities between them. But there are a number of general issues which have formed a particular focus for discussion and debate in the search for an explanation. In particular:

- how best to define genocide
- how to categorise different kinds of genocide
- how to think about the kinds of societies and states in which genocide occurs
- whether to think of genocide as largely a 'top-down' process, driven by state elites, or more as the (not necessarily intended) outcome of complex social dynamics

- whether to think about genocide as a process that unfolds over time, or as a decision made by leaders that is then realised
- how to think about the purposes of elites when they decide on genocide
- how to think about the ideologies embraced by genocidal elites and their followers
- how to think about the wider context, and in particular the significance of war, ethnic conflict, empire and the nation state.

These issues have been addressed in a variety of ways, as a range of different writers have attempted to provide explanations for why genocide recurs. Whatever their differences, however, they generally agree with Lemkin that genocide has to be understood as a modern crime which differs from earlier forms of mass killing. Not only is genocide not confined to killing, but the destruction it involves is committed by states with significant resources at their disposal, operating in a global order structured in a particular fashion. It occurs in complex societies, composed of various groups, shaped and divided in different ways. As a crime of our time, it demands to be understood, and not just as an academic question. Very few who write about it do so entirely dispassionately and without some hope that, with more knowledge, it might be possible to do more to stop it recurring.

## Pioneers – Leo Kuper and Helen Fein

This was certainly the case for the man often regarded after Lemkin as the pioneer of genocide studies, Leo Kuper. A South African émigré from apartheid, Kuper produced what is generally regarded as the first major work on the topic. With some reservations, Kuper accepted the Convention's definition of genocide, largely because it had been legally accepted. He distinguished between two different kinds of genocide – one 'domestic', the other occurring in the context of war. His major concern was with the former, which he saw as the product of plural societies unable to cope with internal divisions of ethnicity, religion or 'race'. 'The plural society provides', Kuper argued, 'the structural basis for genocide', where there are what he called 'persistent and pervasive cleavages', upon which are superimposed systematic inequalities.[3] Already in 1981, he was worried about the prospects of further genocides, particularly in the context of decolonisation, drawing attention to what had happened in Biafra, the Sudan and Bangladesh (see Chapters 5 and 7). He argued that many imperialist powers had created unstable pluralist entities which could not hang together in the longer term. The temptation would be for one group to turn to genocide to assert its power over others.

The mere fact of plurality, however, is not enough on its own to generate genocide, since there are many pluralist societies where no genocide has taken place. For that to happen, Helen Fein, another pioneer in the field, argued it was necessary for states to have a plan of action. Extending the Convention's definition (although she urged using it whenever possible), Fein saw it as

> sustained purposeful action by a perpetrator to physically destroy a collectivity directly or indirectly, through interdiction of the biological and social reproduction of group members, sustained regardless of the surrender or lack of threat offered by the victim.[4]

By highlighting 'physical destruction', she emphasised killing more than the Convention actually does. But by also stressing the question of reproduction, she opened the way too for what was later to become an important line of enquiry into the role of sexual violence in genocide (see Chapter 4).

## Purposes

Both forms of destruction, however, were intended. They were the result of 'purposeful action' by perpetrators. Their specific purposes might vary because not all genocides were exactly the same. Fein distinguished between four kinds.

- In *developmental genocide*, the purpose is to gain control of an area, eliminating groups who prevent its full possession and exploitation.
- In *despotic genocide*, the aim is to destroy groups which represent an actual or potential obstacle to the enjoyment of total power.
- In *retributive genocide*, the motive has to do with experience or fear of another group's hostile action.
- In *ideological genocide*, there is a utopian vision for society in which the targeted group has no place.

In a wide-ranging study that went further back than 1945, Frank Chalk and Kurt Jonassohn also linked types of genocide to motives, but classified them slightly differently. In their view, there were:

- genocides which sought to eliminate a perceived threat
- genocides designed to spread terror among real or potential enemies
- genocides where the aim was to acquire economic wealth
- genocides where the purpose was to implement a belief, theory or ideology.

It was the last of these which they thought was becoming increasingly the dominant form, and is one of the reasons why they saw the exclusion of political groups from the Convention as such a problem. Arguing that, for the purposes of genocide, the group existed primarily in the mind of the perpetrator, they defined it as 'a form of one-sided mass killing in which a state or other authority intends to destroy a group, as that group and membership in it are defined by the perpetrator'.[5]

The one-sidedness of genocide is a central issue for another pioneer, Israel Charny, who fought hard to raise the question of genocide at a time when it was not seen by many as a major problem. His acute awareness of the vulnerability of victims lies at the heart of his own redefinition of genocide as 'the mass killing of substantial numbers of human beings when not in the course of a military action against the military forces of an avowed enemy, under conditions of the essential defencelessness and hopelessness of the victim'.[6] Charny's emphasis in this definition on the weakness and vulnerability of victim groups is very important, particularly when it comes to thinking about what is to be done to help victims, as we shall see later in this book.

## Genocide as problem-solving

But clearly it is also important to explain why perpetrators think it makes sense to destroy a group in the first place, although this is by no means a question Charny ignores. Following Fein to some extent, Benjamin Valentino and Manus Midlarsky see perpetrators as rational actors who, having considered various options to achieve their goals, opt for genocide. This is a largely political interpretation, as opposed to one which stresses social divisions. The problem with the latter, as Valentino sees it, is that genocide occurs not only in plural and divided societies but also in relatively homogeneous ones.

Defining genocide as 'the intentional mass killings of non-combatants' of 50,000 or more, Valentino argues that they are 'final solutions' to what appear to elites as problems which cannot be solved any other way. He views mass killing as essentially instrumental, 'a brutal strategy designed to accomplish leaders' most important ideological and political objectives and counter what they see as their most dangerous threats'.[7] In China and in Cambodia, genocide followed the model established by the Soviet Union. It was the end result of a communist project for the whole society which brooked no opposition. The killing of the Tutsi in Rwanda followed the model adopted for the Jews by the Nazis, and for the Armenians by the Young Turks; it was the final solution chosen after pressure to force them to leave failed to achieve its end.

The killing of indigenous groups in Guatemala was the end result of a counter-insurgency project. Internal insurgency, however, is not the only threat to states. Resources and territory can be lost to other states too and it is this loss which, according to Midlarsky, can be a particular motivation for genocide, as elites seek to compensate for loss of power, resources, status and rank (a point also made by Fein).[8]

## Ideology

A slightly different approach to the intent to commit genocide has been taken by Eric Weitz, who, like Frank Chalk, places more emphasis on ideology. Weitz argues compellingly that there are some ways of thinking about the world which have led elites, particularly in the twentieth century, to be prepared to embrace 'final solutions'. These come from ideas about race and about the nation which developed in the West in the nineteenth and twentieth centuries, drawing on beliefs about progress and a supposedly 'scientific' way of thinking about the world. The idea of race had already been used to justify slavery and the extreme violence committed against indigenous peoples by Western states. Now it was used to transform understandings of the nation itself. The nation became 'racialised' and thought about in biological terms as a body which needed to be made clean and pure. These ideas were used to generate utopian and revolutionary schemes of one kind or another, 'powerful visions of the future'.[9] If the nation was to become strong and successful, it was necessary to eliminate groups which supposedly held it back or undermined it or conspired against it. Weitz argues that such schemes became much more prevalent in the twentieth century, particularly after the First World War.

## Genocide, revolution and war

Others have made revolution and war a central focus of their explanation of genocide. Robert Melson, for example, argues that ideology comes to play a crucial role in genocide in the context provided by revolution and war, as in the Armenian, Jewish, Cambodian and Rwandan cases.[10] Certain kinds of revolutionary ideology do seem to provide answers to some people in societies shaken by war. Omer Bartov sees the First World War as decisive in this respect. It ushered in a century of extreme violence, rooted in acute anxieties about identity, which became fatally politicised. Concerns about who is and who is not to be trusted, about who 'we' are or should be, were then 'grafted onto conventional struggles for power and hegemony',[11] generating apocalyptic solutions of one kind or another, not only in Nazi Germany but elsewhere in Cambodia, in Rwanda, for example (see Chapters 4 and 5).

An even more systematic effort to explain genocide in connection with war has been made by Martin Shaw. Seeking to understand it sociologically, as a form of social action, Shaw sees it as 'social destruction, of a people and their way of life'.[12] It is the outcome of a process involving conflictual social relations, embedded in structures in which power is unevenly and asymmetrically distributed and deployed. Nowhere is this more likely than in war, and Shaw defines genocide specifically as 'a particular form of modern warfare, and an extension of the more common form of *degenerate* war'.[13] During the course of the last two centuries, modern war has in his view become transformed. The First World War saw states mobilising whole societies for war, not just with mass conscription but organising production to provide what was essential for the war effort as a whole. Unarmed civilians in enemy societies now became strategic targets themselves. The Second World War was even more brutal and unrestrained, with a massive increase in civilian casualties as whole groups were targeted.

War is certainly an ideal cover for genocide. If war does not simply cause genocide (an important point Shaw insists on), it creates and legitimates a climate of violence in which hatred and fear of the enemy are mobilised and openly expressed. States direct propaganda against an enemy, who they frequently depict in dehumanised terms. They acquire more and more power, much of it often secret because of the supposed needs of war itself. They use armies and other paramilitary organisations to attack not only other armed combatants but increasingly vulnerable civilians too, also seen as the enemy. As the scope of conflict has widened, as the stakes in conflict have risen, war is being waged not just against other armies but against whole societies, to demolish the infrastructure which sustains the competitor. Civilians have thus become direct targets for states.

## Ethnic cleansing

One difficulty with this approach is that Lemkin and the Convention both insisted that genocide could take place in times of peace as well as in times of war. Not all wars even in the twentieth century have involved genocide, and genocides have sometimes taken place not during war but afterwards, as in Cambodia. There is also the issue, raised in Helen Fein's definition, that it is not just a question of an unequal context; genocides are also launched against groups which were no threat at all in the first place, and cannot seriously be seen as military enemies of any kind. The Jews were clearly no threat to the Nazi state, nor did unarmed Cambodian city dwellers pose any challenge to the Khmer Rouge.

One answer to this is that it does not matter. The issue is not whether a group *is* a threat but whether it is perceived or constructed *as* a threat. This is particularly the case when we come to think about ethnic groups, who are the focus of Michael Mann's explanation of genocide. Like Kuper, Mann looks at divisions in society, in this case ethnic ones. Like Fein, he argues that the mere fact that ethnic differences exist is not by itself the problem. They have to be made to *seem* critical and intolerable by radical groups competing with each other for support. This is a political question because it is about power and control over territory to which two groups are laying serious and usually long-standing claims. One side resorts to genocide, according to Mann, when it thinks it can remove the other ('cleanse' it) from the contested area without serious cost to itself. This is a multi-layered account, in which there is a complex interplay between elites and social groups, and between the contending groups. The outcome is a result of multiple interactions, encompassing a large number of people at different levels. Participation in the genocidal process is widespread, with initiatives coming as much from below as from above, in a context of unfolding and deepening crisis. Genocide is not the predictable end product of a clearly worked out plan but a contingent outcome of a complex set of social and political processes.

One distinguishing feature of this account is the question Mann raises about the link between genocide and democracy. Genocide occurs, Mann argues, when the question of who is or should be included in the people (the *demos*) becomes a critical issue. Differing conceptions emerge as answers, some requiring particular groups to be eliminated or 'cleansed' from the 'people'. The attempt to connect genocide to what Mann calls the 'dark side of democracy' is not entirely persuasive, however, since at least two of the cases he discusses, Nazi Germany and the Soviet Russia, were hardly societies in transition to democracy.

## Genocide, colonialism and empire

The killings in the Soviet Union of course had effectively been excluded from the Convention, with Lemkin's agreement.[14] In recent years, however, there has been some reconsideration of what Lemkin himself had been thinking. As Michael McDonnell and Dirk Moses and John

Docker have shown, Lemkin had been working for some time before his untimely death in 1959 on a wide-ranging history of genocide in which colonialism figured prominently.[15] Lemkin was following up a critical point he had made in his definition of the genocidal process, where he had referred to 'the colonisation of the area by the oppressor's own nationals'.[16] Lemkin looked at the behaviour of Spanish colonisers in Latin America, where he estimated that some 20 million South American Indians were killed, not including those who died from exploitation. In his projected history, there were going to be sections on genocides committed by the Germans against the Hereros in Africa, by the Belgians in the Congo, by the British against the Maoris in New Zealand, and against Aboriginals in Tasmania and elsewhere in Australia. He also made notes about genocide in North America, resulting from the colonisers' dispossession and enslavement of indigenous peoples, as well as direct killings.

Alongside all this killing, Lemkin focused again on the issue of cultural genocide which had been dropped, to his dismay, from the Convention. He identified various methods through which whole cultures were destroyed, including the elimination of group leadership, forced conversion to another set of beliefs, the prohibition of cultural activities, the destruction of symbols and cultural centres and systematic looting. He understood clearly how the elimination of a core group can have devastating effects and how cultural destruction can be hard to recover from, particularly if the memory of what has disappeared is lost or systematically repressed. Lemkin's concern with culture, as McDonnell and Moses suggest, may have been too limited to high culture and he had also perhaps too uncritical a view of assimilation,[17] not seeing the way that this too can lead, not so innocently, to the disappearance of cultures over time, but the issues he raised have become of increasing importance to our understanding of genocide.

Looking again at Lemkin in this light has clearly stimulated a new approach to explaining genocide. A number of writers have argued that some of the explanations we have looked at so far suffer from a serious blindness to precisely the connections Lemkin identified between empire, colony and genocide. Preoccupied by what went on in Europe in the twentieth century, when white Europeans killed other white Europeans, they have fatally ignored the much greater toll of destruction wrought by Europeans outside Europe for centuries on those they dispossessed, colonised, enslaved and murdered. The reason for this blindness, Dirk Moses for example has argued, stems from a liberal bias, a frame of reference which assumes that it is non-liberal states and societies which are likely to be the problem. In fact, liberal societies and states themselves have been heavily involved in genocidal processes for centuries.[18]

One important reason for this blindness, Moses argues, is the way in which the Holocaust has sometimes been thought about as unique, or as quite separate from other genocides, or as the paradigm case. Rather than seeing it in these ways, it can be helpful to situate the Holocaust within a broader frame of reference. Genocide (as Lemkin realised) significantly predated the Holocaust. It might even help to think about the Holocaust as yet another case of genocide brought about by imperialist annexation and colonial ambition.[19] It took place after all in Eastern Europe, where the German state was seeking to expand its empire, having abandoned earlier efforts to seize colonies abroad.

There are several problems with this approach, not least that it is not easy to see how a desire to annihilate the entire Jewish people (not exactly white Europeans) was a necessary part of a strategy of imperial conquest. Nevertheless, this wider frame of reference can be used to open the way to rethinking genocide since 1945. Rather than simply following the Holocaust, from which so many genocides turn out to differ in specific details, they could also be understood as continued effects of European colonisation.

## The case of Australia – genocide against indigenous peoples

One case which spans the period before and after 1945 is Australia. Indigenous peoples, composed of many different groups and speaking nearly 300 different languages, had lived there undisturbed for up to 125,000 years before the first ships of colonists arrived from England in 1788. Indigenous peoples today constitute at most 2.5 per cent of the population; few of the groups or their languages or their different cultures survive. The majority probably died from diseases brought in by the colonisers or from malnutrition as they were deprived of access to the natural resources that had sustained them before. Many though were also massacred in 'frontier wars' sparked by settlers' efforts to annex land, which was conveniently defined by the British as '*terra nullius*' or 'land belonging to no one'.

This violence was justified by a racist discourse in which 'Aboriginals' (perceived as one single group) were described as vermin and in which it was assumed that they should and would disappear quite quickly. The destruction, however, was not merely physical but cultural. There were sustained efforts to remove indigenous children from their groups and bring them up as white Australians, a policy sometimes described as 'breeding out the colour'. This went on long after the killing had stopped, into the 1950s, even (if one includes policies of fostering and adoption) into the 1970s and 1980s. Similar policies were pursued in Canada over the same period. It is hard not to see this falling within the category of the act defined in the Convention as 'forcibly transferring children of the group to another group' or even as a 'measure which prevented births within the group'.

In 1997, a national enquiry indeed concluded, dramatically, that this was a case of genocide. There has subsequently been a considerable debate in Australia about whether all or some or none of this was genocide.[20] It can be argued that the intent behind the policy of removing children was not malign but it was clearly guided by racist assumptions, that indigenous peoples were inferior and bound to disappear, and ambitions that this process be hastened.[21]

It can be argued more generally that there was no intent to destroy the indigenous groups. The outcome though, as in many other parts of the world, was that they almost completely disappeared. It is true that the instructions to the first governor general were 'to live in kindness' with the local population. However, this approach did not survive much contact with the indigenous population once they realised that the colonists wanted to seize their land and resources and they began, against what was in the end overwhelming force, to resist.

It has even been argued that indigenous peoples in Australia have not disappeared entirely, but this ignores the fact that the Convention refers to destruction in part as well as in whole. Even if genocide does not characterise the whole of Australian history, there have nevertheless been a significant number of what Moses calls 'genocidal moments'.[22] They came about when the colonisers were faced with resistance, when indigenous peoples rebelled against their new masters, in Australia as in many other places. These were not accidents but have to be understood in the context of a structure created by imperial annexation and colonisation.

The issues raised in the debates about what happened in Australia clearly go much further and wider than this one case. They have to do with the relative significance to be attached to structure or agency, to intent or outcome, to mass killing or cultural destruction. They raise too the question of whether genocide should be conceived of as an event or set of events, or as an unfolding, dynamic process, and how this process itself might be connected to, or distinguished from, other, broader processes and developments.

One of the most important of such developments has been settler-colonialism. Patrick Wolfe has argued that many genocides, if not all, have to be understood in this context, because contests for land are so often contests for life. If settler-colonialism is not invariably genocidal, it is inherently so, and a major 'indicator', because it follows what he calls a 'logic of elimination'.[23] When one group of people wants to take another's land, they will pursue a variety of strategies which are likely to result in the latter's destruction as a group. This often involves racism, as one group seeks space for its 'race',[24] although not all groups are racialised in the same way or for the same ends. Black people, for example, were racialised as slaves, whose labour was needed; native Americans as 'Indians' whose land was being seized. Their removal was achieved through a variety of complementary strategies. There was killing on the frontier, often wildly by settlers whose actions were then legitimated and backed up by an imperial state which may not have ordered this violence at all in the first place but whose invasion and claim to sovereignty over the land created the conditions for it. Indigeneous peoples could constantly be forced on and back. When there was no more space left for them to go to, a strategy of assimilation could then be deployed – a move from the maxim 'the only good Indian is a dead Indian' to 'kill the Indian in him and save the man'.[25] (Assimilation, however, was not without serious consequences for life expectancy itself.) What linked the two was that collective, tribal indigenous ownership was replaced by settler-colonial control of land for the production on a world market. Individual members of indigenous peoples could become part of this process but only by abandoning their identity and culture.

Wolfe's sharp focus on land and labour is one way of connecting genocide to empire and colony, with consequences that stretch on into the post-1945 period. As he points out, the machetes used by Hutus to murder Tutsis in Rwanda are the same tools they used to produce goods for the world market; (some) Tutsi land ownership was, as we shall see, a structural factor in the Rwandan genocide (see Chapter 6).[26] But there is also the question of colonial rule itself, which has also itself often been genocidal as imperialist states waged total war on the populations they invaded. To the many cases Lemkin identified can be added those of the French in Algeria and the British in Kenya, both of which occurred after 1945.

The obvious problem with this connection is that not all colonial rule, clearly, *was* genocidal. There is no evidence of either genocidal intent or outcome in, for example, Hong Kong or India, and in several other cases. One response to this objection is to suggest, as Dirk Moses has done, that 'the greater the intensity of colonial rule, the greater the likelihood of genocide'.[27] He ties this, amongst other things, to security concerns, which arose when imperial powers met resistance which had to be crushed or feared losing control, especially on the periphery.

(Here his argument meshes with Valentino's analysis of genocide as a consequence of counter-insurgency strategies.)[28]

The connection between empire, colony and genocide is easier to see before 1945, when the world was largely divided up between imperialist powers, not all of them Western by any means. (The Soviet Union, a serial perpetrator in its own right, can in many ways be seen as the successor to the Tsarist Russian Empire; imperialism more generally long predated the rise of Western states.) A major development after 1945 was decolonisation, the result of widespread and prolonged struggles against colonial rule.

The question that then arises is what happened after the colonisers departed?

## Empire, colony and genocide after 1945

One answer is that the colonisers did not always depart but continued the process of destruction, culturally but also physically. In control of most of the wealth and resources, they have continued to conceive of indigenous peoples not only as inferior but as an inherent threat to the social order they have constructed or are still building (as in the case of Guatemala discussed in Chapter 5).

Alternatively, if the colonisers did depart, there are the genocides Kuper drew attention to, which occurred in the context of decolonisation. Had it not been for colonisation in the first place which created artificial societies and for the colonisers' policy of divide and rule, the resentments, fears and grievances which generated genocide would not have existed. Genocide, on this account, does not occur because these societies are illiberal or are unable to manage tensions inherent in any plural society. It occurs because colonialism has generated these tensions in the first place and created a structure within which they cannot be contained.

Third, there are cases where imperialist powers (whether or not they were direct colonisers in the first place) have colluded with and facilitated genocides. They have done so because they have major interests in who holds power in societies with resources they continue to exploit. In Latin America especially but also in part of Asia, the United States has been charged with supporting, if not helping to organise genocides undertaken by local elites (see Chapter 5).

There is though another side to this. Some rebellions against local elites or colonisers can also become genocidal in their turn. These can be seen as cases of what Adam Jones and Nicholas Robins have called 'subaltern genocide'.[29] Here, it is argued, previously oppressed groups turn upon those who were either their colonial tormentors or colluded with them and benefitted from their favours (or were believed to have done so, which is not always or exactly the same thing). This line of argument is an important development in several respects, and can be used to illuminate some of what happened in Cambodia and Rwanda (see Chapters 4 and 5). It provides further evidence of the destructive impact of imperial annexation and colonisation, as previously subjugated groups resorted in their turn to extreme violence. It raises difficult ethical questions too, as Jones has bravely acknowledged, about where or how to distinguish (if at all) between legitimate or understandable violent resistance against oppression and the crime of genocide.[30] But these very questions draw our attention back to the identity and active agency of those committing genocide and the choices they make, which can perhaps be minimised if there is too great a focus on the structural conditions created by empire and colony.

## The post-colonial nation state and nationalism

If in the period of direct imperial rule and colonisation, it was often non-state actors who turned to genocide, it has generally been elites in control of post-colonial states who have been the immediate perpetrators since 1945, often (and ironically) counting on the collusion or assistance of their former masters.

The structure within which post-colonial elites operate may have been bequeathed to them by imperialism but is one within which they can carve out their own space and pursue their own interests. From one angle, their genocidal actions can be seen to be following a practice developed long ago by their colonialist predecessors, who committed genocide not only abroad but much closer to home, even at home. This argument has been advanced most systematically by Mark Levene, and in an even more ambitious way by Christopher Powell. Levene argues that the contemporary international system within which all states operate, including post-colonial newcomers, is an inherently competitive and violent one. It was established in the first instance by Western states, who not only raided and exploited other territory and peoples, commandeering vital material resources to fight off their rivals but were also engaged in a process of internal homogenisation. This was often genocidal, as they destroyed all alternate sources of power within their borders, and secured the obedience and loyalty of their own subjects. Among the examples he cites are the French in the Vendée in 1793–4 in the course of the Revolution, and also the English in 'pacifying' the Scottish highlands earlier in the century.[31] Newcomers are as vulnerable as the original Western nation states once were and could be seen as essentially following their example, fearing internal division, divided loyalties or even secession. This approach could explain some of what occurred in Yugoslavia and Iraq in the late 1980s and 1990s (see Chapter 6).

Powell goes further still, arguing that the creation of a global system of nation states was a crucial part of the development of Western civilisation itself. Genocide, rather than being a product of an apocalyptic scenario, as others have suggested, has actually been made possible, even likely, by the civilising process. On the one hand, as nation states monopolised power, they created spaces within which violence appears at first sight to recede. On the other hand, the capacity for violence actually increased, because the means of violence were now reproduced on a larger scale.[32]

The role of nationalism in genocide may make even more sense in this framework. (Powell sees imperialism and nationalism coming to 'fruition' jointly.)[33] As the ideology which accompanied the formation of the original nation states, it has been repeatedly invoked by genocidal perpetrators, identifying enemies of the nation within and without. Several post-colonial states, as we shall see, have embraced this ideology with a vengeance. Although nationalism can clearly take many different forms, and is not always genocidal, it can easily become so when it is combined with other elements. It is hard to find examples of genocidal ideology since 1945 where nationalism has not been a crucial ingredient. In his wide-ranging history of genocide, Ben Kiernan gives several examples of genocides occurring when an ambitious nationalism, with forward-looking aspirations to both unchallenged rule and territorial expansion, has been combined with backward-looking components, cults of antiquity and a preoccupation with land and agricultural settlement.[34]

## 'Alien' elements

Kiernan's view may have been partly forged by his extensive research into the Cambodia case, which has also been the focus of Alexander Hinton's increasingly influential anthropological approach to genocide.[35] Hinton and others have shown that elites can be very good at manipulating local cultural traditions. It is important though to see that culture is often reified and made to appear as if it is fixed and certain, when it is a process, fluid and always changing as people come and go, live and work and interact. (One of the problems with Lemkin's understanding of culture, deriving from his largely primordialist conception of groups, especially national ones,[36] is that it does not leave space for hybridity and adaptation.)[37]

In the discourse of the architects of genocide, arguments that a particular 'alien' group by its very presence and existence threatens this reified culture often play a prominent role. An important aspect of this, as Kiernan argues, is a construction of a mythical past, in which the targeted group were supposedly not present, when the nation was strong and powerful, before it became weakened and polluted by foreign elements. For Jacques Sémelin, destruction always has this purifying justification, fuelled by a desire to annihilate what is seen to be unclean or dirty in some way.[38]

The project of purification, however, can go beyond one particular group. Daniel Feierstein has suggested that genocide needs to be thought of as a 'social practice' which both destroys and reorganises the whole of society.[39] It breaks up solidarity between citizens, and fatally undermines the ethics of mutual recognition, respect and reciprocity. The great strength of this approach is that it reminds us that the effects of genocide are felt everywhere, by everyone – not just by victims or perpetrators but those who stand by and allow their fellow citizens to be removed from their community.

### Destruction and omnipotence

Although Feierstein does not argue that all genocides are the same, he does suggest that the idea of reorganising the whole of society, a project of national reconstruction, is characteristic of the second half of the twentieth century, beginning with the Nazis. In this sense he returns us to the Holocaust, that radical event which led to the Convention in the first place.

Here, there has been an important debate in recent years about a question of timing which might appear to be rather technical but may carry a deeper significance for our understanding of how genocide is decided upon. In a detailed study of the radicalisation of Nazi policy towards the Jews, Christopher Browning has argued that the decision to exterminate the Jews was taken not, as some others have suggested, when they were facing major crises or any prospect of ultimate defeat but in what he calls a 'moment of euphoria', when the Nazi elite believed they were on the verge of total triumph.[40]

If this interpretation is right, it may have implications for thinking about genocide more generally. It may be that it is this sense, that the world *can now* be reshaped according to their beliefs about how it should look, that is common to the architects of genocide. The vulnerable group would then appear to them at that moment as weak and defenceless (as Charny, and Chalk and Johansson emphasised). Within the borders of the sovereign state, as it seeks to fortify itself and compete (Levene's argument), or in the context of war when the state has become so powerful (Shaw's argument), there is no other power that can prevent them from destroying the targeted group. There appears to be no restrictions on what can then be done, since the targeted group is too weak to resist and external forces will not come to their aid. There may be different fantasies, racist or nationalist (as Weitz argued), inherited or inverted from colonialism (according to anti-imperialist and subaltern theorists), about what the world will then look like. There may be different groups who pose obstacles in the way of their realisation – 'problems' that require 'solutions' (to use Valentino's language). They are, however, all fantasies which can be implemented because there seems to be nothing to prevent them from being so.

It may be the sense that there are no such restraints that can help explain the decision to commit genocide. At the point at which the decision is made, the sense that the fantasy can after all *be* implemented may be critical to the decision itself. It might be thought about in terms of *omnipotence*, a belief that anything can now be done to a target group which now lies at the mercy of the potential perpetrator. In some ways, this is what Hannah Arendt identified as the break involved in the Holocaust, that there were now people who felt no restraints upon them, something that she traced back to the perceptions and behaviour of European imperialists operating far away from the laws and restraints of the metropole.[41] The same sense that anything is possible, that the world really can be re-engineered from top to bottom is present too in Zygmunt Bauman's interpretation of the Holocaust (and by extension other genocides too) as a modern phenomenon when those in control of modern states imagine the world, as he puts it, as a 'garden' which they will design from scratch and clear of all 'weeds'.[42]

This sense of limitless possibility is not irreconcilable with arguments that perpetrators of genocide have fears or deep resentments towards the other, which drive them to want to eliminate them. Fear and resentment is, in many ways, the reverse side of omnipotence, which aims to render them null and void. They may be aroused for different reasons (see also Chapter 4). They may be aroused because of perceived past treatment, (as subaltern theorists argue). They may be aroused for entirely fabricated reasons in relation to a mythologised past, where the perpetrators' own group had been all-powerful once (as Kiernan has suggested). Either way, omnipotence can be thought about as an insistence that what is feared or resented can be made not to matter. It can now be destroyed in whole or in part, enough that it will never trouble again.

On this argument, those who decide upon genocide are emboldened to do so, because they think (too often rightly) that there is no one, or not enough, who will prevent them. They adopt their 'final solution' at some level because they can, because there are no obstacles in their way.

If this is right, however, we still need to know how and why there are so few obstacles in their way. How are perpetrators found and mobilised? How do victims react? Why do others ('bystanders') let the destruction take place? But, also, why do some others ('rescuers') intervene?

# 4 Perpetrators, bystanders, victims and rescuers

Genocide is not, of course, the work of only a few people. The destruction of a group in whole or in part requires extensive participation, sometimes involving alarmingly high numbers. This raises some very difficult issues. Some of these are *organisational*, since genocide is not a random event. Some are *psychological,* to do with the motivations of groups and individuals. Some are *contextual*, to do with the cultural settings and the political, social and economic circumstances within which people make their choices.

Again, these issues have been addressed from various perspectives. Before considering them further here, however, it is important to see that the question of participation is not confined only to perpetrators. The great Holocaust historian Raul Hilberg argued that there are three parties to genocide – not just perpetrators and their victims but also bystanders (see Figure 4.1).[1] There is, however, also another category, that of rescuers. Rather than a triangle, therefore, it may be better to think of a continuum, with perpetrators at one end and rescuers at the other, and bystanders in the middle. These are, moreover, not necessarily fixed positions (see Figure 4.2). It is possible, it seems, for people to be perpetrators at one moment, bystanders another and even rescuers another.[2]

## Perpetrators

### *States – totalitarian or modern?*

Genocide occurs largely in an organisational context provided by states, although that does not mean that participation has to be explained as a top-down matter. But it does raise the question nevertheless, touched upon in the last chapter, of whether genocide is possible in only some kinds of states.

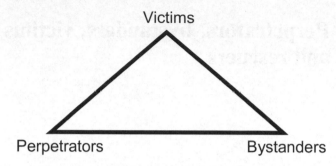

*Figure 4.1*

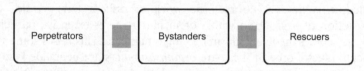

*Figure 4.2*

Both Irving Louis Horowitz and R. J. Rummel think that genocides are much more likely in authoritarian or totalitarian states.[3] In Rummel's view,

> Fundamentally, genocide is a product of the type of government a country has. ... Modern democratic governments have committed virtually no domestic genocide. Those governments that commit the most genocide have been totalitarian governments, while those that committed lesser genocide have been partially or wholly authoritarian and dictatorial.[4]

There are reasons why totalitarian states might be able to kill such huge numbers. They are single party dictatorships, which destroy all organised opposition; they deploy powerful repressive forces, secret police and paramilitary organisations which terrorise the population into passivity and compliance; they propagate monolithic ideologies which demand complete adherence.

There are several possible difficulties with this line of argument. It can be argued, for instance, that it is too trapped within a liberal frame of reference[5] and that not all genocidal states appear to have been totalitarian. Rather than totalitarianism then, there may be something about the modern state more generally which makes genocide possible. Perhaps it has something to do with the way in which the modern state possesses legitimacy in the eyes of its citizens, and in which people obey its rules, laws and commands. The modern state not only possesses a monopoly of the means of coercion. It also commands the loyalty of its subjects through a variety of mechanisms. Some of these are ideological, fostering a 'common sense' that 'we' are all part of one national community – an identity 'flagged' through events, commemorations and the educational system.[6] Some are organisational, as the state provides the security and stability necessary for social life, the rules, processes and procedures which people abide by on a day-to-day basis.

However, many state organisations also play an important role in genocide – not only the obviously coercive ones, such as the police or the army, but also administrative ones, such as the civil service. These organisations provide some of the crucial structures within which perpetrators are effectively licensed to carry out genocide.

## *Armies and paramilitaries*

In several cases of genocide, armies and paramilitaries have played a central role.[7] Generals have often been among the key perpetrators, able to rely on their soldiers to carry out their orders, knowing that they are trained in ways that helped prepare them for what they want them to do. Soldiers generally have to be ready for combat, to be prepared to engage in violence, to become experts in killing, to follow orders given by their superiors. They may see killing and destruction as an inevitable, unavoidable consequence of the combat situation in which they find themselves. They will not necessarily have an overview which would even allow them to see that they are carrying out genocide. This is not a defence of course. Orders to carry out genocide should be disobeyed, as courts have insisted, and some armies now include in their training manuals references to this issue. But the very fact that they have felt compelled to do so may be an indication of the extent of potential military involvement in genocide.

Every state has a professional army but not every state has paramilitaries, who also figure prominently in many genocides. There are important distinctions between the two, even when armies are expanded to include conscripts. Paramilitaries do not have the same rationale, formation or purpose. Often they are brought into being in order to mobilise more people than armies can easily do and to undertake tasks that soldiers would prefer not to be seen to be performing. The people who join paramilitary organisations are not subject to the same training and do not operate within similar formal hierarchies. This has the distinct advantage for state elites bent on genocide that it can then be harder to trace back responsibility. Political leaders can then argue disingenuously that they knew nothing about what paramilitaries were doing. It is clear in cases of genocide, however, that paramilitaries (as in Rwanda and Bosnia, for example) are mobilised by elites on the basis of an overt call to commit violence. The generally young men who enlist are inculcated from the outset in a spirit of hatred, and operate in a subculture in which cruelty and torture rapidly become established norms (see Chapter 6).

There are also special forces, on the edge of the army or police, like the *Mukhabarat* in Iraq (see Chapter 5). Here the issue is less a more immediately mobilised hatred than what might be called a perverse professionalism, since the 'job' itself usually requires an expertise, if not a sadistic pleasure, in violence designed to terrify, humiliate and dehumanise.

### Bureaucrats and professionals

Cruelty and sadism alone cannot, however, sufficiently explain participation in genocide. An important role is also played by people working in organisations not in any immediate sense devoted to inflicting direct violence, by bureaucrats who draft the processes, procedures and laws, which result in the destruction of large numbers of people. The importance of 'desk murderers' emerged first in the history of the Holocaust, particularly in Raul Hilberg's meticulous reconstruction of the machinery of destruction and the central part played in it by civil servants, lawyers and professionals.[8] Each of these could be seen, from one angle, as simply doing their job 'properly', using their training and expertise to come up with 'solutions' to 'problems' given them by their political masters.

Zygmunt Bauman has argued that this aspect of genocide shows how it has to be understood as an intrinsically modern phenomenon.[9] Bureaucracies develop rules and procedures which apply not to individuals but to cases or classes. They are grounded in an instrumental rationality which seeks to find the best way to get from A to B, not considering the more fundamental question of whether B is the right thing to be aiming at in the first place – genocide in this case. Bauman also points to the critical distance between professionals and the objects of their policies and processes. Their victims often remain personally unknown, because they are distant, remote, far away. The consequences for real, living human beings are very often not witnessed by those who construct the detailed plans, processes and rules which result in their destruction. (This is not, however, always the case. As we shall see, in both Bosnia and Rwanda, an important aspect of the killing was its face-to-face character, although this does not necessarily mean it was any less modern in other vital respects. This has led some to criticise Baumann for a too narrow, even Eurocentric approach,[10] in which the Holocaust looms too large as an ideal type.)

There does not, in any event, always have to be this distance for professionals to insulate themselves from the moral consequences of their genocidal actions. Robert Lifton conducted a famous study of Nazi doctors, who carried out terrifying experiments and played a key role in deciding who was to live and who was to be killed.[11] Lifton found that the insulation involved a kind of 'doubling' in which there could effectively be two selves – one continuing to hold on to the traditional values of the medical profession; the other which had internalised genocidal norms. The existence of these two selves, quite separate from each other, allowed doctors to dissociate, to remain 'sane' enough to work as professionals in a genocidal context. This 'doubling' meant that they could avoid any significant sense of guilt for what they were doing. Lifton's argument is not, however, necessarily restricted to doctors; it can be applied to many other professionals involved in genocide.

There has been some debate about this explanation. James Waller has suggested that 'doubling, rather than a *cause* of evildoing, can easily be seen as a *consequence*. In other words, it is an adaptation that does not explain *how* ordinary people commit extraordinary evil, only how they cope with their participation in evildoing once it has commenced'.[12] But the problem goes beyond professionals. If these people, educated, successful, skilled, can become involved in genocide and silence their doubts (if they have any), what about those who carry out genocide directly?

### *Ordinary men?*

Most of the debate about perpetrators has focused on this question. The debate has largely been between those who think that only certain kinds of people, with particular *dispositions,* are perpetrators of genocide, against those who think that genocidal violence is rooted in the *situation* in which quite ordinary people find themselves.

The 'dispositional' approach looks for evidence that perpetrators are somehow abnormal or pathological. It was followed immediately after the war with a series of interviews with Nazi leaders but these did not reveal anything especially unusual about them, contrary to expectations.[13] A more substantial study conducted in the United States in the late 1940s claimed, however, that there was something which could be identified as an 'Authoritarian Personality'.[14] The authors developed what they called the 'F scale', a personality test designed to measure authoritarian tendencies. The answers appeared to show that certain people had a set of traits which predisposed them to follow a strong leader and accept orders unquestioningly. Although influential for a time, it then came in for considerable criticism. Some of this had to do with scepticism about the psychoanalytic theory used to underpin the argument, but there were also difficulties with the apparent assumption that authoritarianism is only a right-wing phenomenon, which would make it difficult to explain a case such as Cambodia (see Chapter 5).

A very different approach has largely dominated the literature, particularly following a series of remarkable experiments conducted in the 1960s by Stanley Milgram in New Haven, Connecticut. These were designed to test how far people would go in obeying authority. A group of people selected from the general population were instructed to punish another group of supposed learners (in fact, actors) with electric shocks every time they made a mistake. The shocks were increased one level at a time, up to a level marked 'danger: severe shock'. An alarmingly high percentage of participants (65 per cent) were willing to go to the two highest levels. The experiments have been repeated subsequently several times in various forms and with largely the same results.

Milgram completed his original experiments just before an Israeli court passed the death sentence on Adolf Eichmann, one of the main organisers of the Holocaust. In her controversial report on Eichmann's trial, Hannah Arendt came to some related conclusions.[15] Taking seriously Eichmann's protestations that he had no ideological animus against Jews, Arendt concluded that the real problem was his inability or refusal to think for himself. He was indeed a bureaucrat, able to commit genocide without realising what he was doing. He was an example of what she called the 'banality of evil'. There was nothing demonic or extraordinary about him at all. On the contrary it was his very ordinariness that was so troubling.

There is, it might seem, nothing unusual about Eichmann and nothing unusual about the ordinary men and women in Milgram's experiments who obeyed authority to such an alarming degree. Anyone put in certain situations might do the same thing. Indeed, this is the conclusion that another Holocaust historian, Christopher Browning, reached in his study of a reserve police battalion in Poland. Browning detected no ideological or sadistic motivation behind their killing day after day of Jews. What he thought was much more important was a combination of routinisation, careerism, peer group pressure and conformity. He specifically referred to Milgram's study to support his own stark conclusion that 'if the men of Reserve Police Battalion 101 could become killers under such circumstances, what group of men cannot?'.[16]

There are, however, a number of possible problems with Milgram's and Arendt's arguments, and their application to the problem of participation in genocide. One is that Eichmann was in fact quite a committed anti-Semite, whose ideology appears to have been more important to him than Arendt recognised. The second is that Milgram's experiments were conducted in a laboratory (obviously) and not in a real-life situation. They did not duplicate what happened in Poland in important respects, or indeed in any other actual genocidal situation, where the victims have been singled out by an ideology as inferior, as less than human and as a mortal threat. Those who followed orders in these experiments generally did not see themselves as genocidal perpetrators, engaged in acts of destruction. In fact many of the participants struggled to some considerable extent with themselves, wanting to be reassured that they were not in fact harming their subjects.

### *Working on emotions*

There may be other or additional reasons for how and why so many people come to feel that it is legitimate and appropriate to do such great harm to others. Daniel Chirot and Clark McCauley argue that a key element is how leaders are able to mobilise certain entirely recognisable and quite ordinary emotions, particularly fear, anger, shame, humiliation, disgust and hate.[17]

With *fear,* for example, perpetrators can be mobilised to envisage those they are destroying as posing a major threat, so that they have to be destroyed before they can carry out what they are supposedly planning. There may also be fear of retribution, after initial acts of destruction have been committed, which enables people to carry on killing once they have started. Fear is of course not only of victims but of others organising the genocide, a point strongly made by Scott Straus in his study of widespread participation in Rwanda.[18] Failure to participate or to show sufficient enthusiasm may be interpreted as disloyalty and put one's own life in serious danger. Those who may have started out trying to save others may then be overwhelmed by fear as the balance of local power shifts towards more committed perpetrators (see Chapter 6). *Anger,* for example, can be evoked by reminding people about supposed past injustice for which genocide can be made to seem retribution. *Shame and humiliation* at the hands of others in the past may evoke a desire for revenge. *Disgust* too may be aroused by

others, they themselves are changed by the experience. Once they begin their work as perpetrators, a kind of escalation effect occurs, as people become socialised into cruelty, and the person merges into the role. Thus 'a person may be quite ordinary in the beginning phase ... only to ultimately become quite extraordinary as a consequence – not a cause – of participation'. It is the participation itself, Waller argues, which makes 'fundamental internal alterations in the psychological framework of the perpetrators ... [H]arming victims can become "normal" behaviour'.[26]

## Bystanders

Staub argues that this is what makes the role of bystanders so important. If there is what he calls 'a continuum of destruction', then bystanders occupy a pivotal position. 'They can define the meaning of events and move others toward empathy or indifference. They can promote values and norms of caring or, by their passivity or participation, they can affirm the perpetrators'.[27] The distinction between perpetrator and bystander is an important one, but it cuts both ways. There is a fundamental difference between carrying out acts of destruction and watching, between commission and omission. However, it is the passivity of others which allows perpetrators to commit the crime, and to carry on doing so, given that genocide is not one single act.

But where are bystanders located and how can they be defined? It is important to remember that genocide does not take place in a completely closed system, but in a global context. Sometimes the most significant bystanders are not located within the society in which genocide is taking place. There are both *internal* and *external* bystanders, and the inaction of those outside may be more important than that of those inside. This raises the question of humanitarian intervention which is taken up in Chapter 7, so the focus here is only on internal actors.

There are several difficulties with understanding the behaviour of bystanders, who after all form the majority in all genocidal situations. One is that it is essentially a counter-factual question, trying to work out what people might have done, rather than what they actually did. To assess this, it is necessary to know what people knew and when they knew it. One classic defence of course is that they did not know and could not have known at the time. A useful distinction here is between what people knew and what people chose not to know.

There is also no one single bystander position. Hilberg himself distinguished between 'onlookers' (those who watched) and 'gainers' (those who benefited directly or indirectly from the despoliation of victims). Greed should certainly not be underestimated as a motive. Indeed perpetrators often engage in looting while they are murdering and terrorising their victims, and bystanders may also see opportunities for themselves as victims are being taken away. In an important sense bystanders actually face two ways – towards perpetrators on the one hand, and toward victims on the other. One choice is whether or not to aid the perpetrators or to avoid becoming one. The other fundamental choice is the inverse of the first – to aid victims or to avoid the danger of becoming one too. This can involve different kinds of action or inaction – to speak up or not, to act overtly or covertly or to remain passive. Again, it is important to see this choice as not necessarily consistent or permanent. People can make different choices at different times, and may be torn about what to do in a succession of situations.

The argument that the action or inaction of bystanders is decisive is not merely rhetorical. There are cases where protest has made a difference. One example (before 1945) is the protest in Germany against the policy of murdering the disabled. This policy, which incidentally enlisted the active participation of many in the medical profession, was stopped because (on one given Sunday) ministers in churches across Germany denounced it, although it is true that it resumed in covert form later. It is also true that this protest did not serve as a model to follow when the genocide of the Jews began. One reason for this is that Jews (unlike many of the disabled) were not Christians. Speaking up for a different group, one reviled for centuries in some Christian traditions, proved more difficult. The prior marginalisation of a group (stressed by Stanton) plays an important part in making it harder for people to protest. But that marginalisation itself cannot happen without wider social acceptance.

What this example points to nevertheless is the fact that, as with perpetrators, it is not necessarily a question of individuals acting in isolation. Bystanders too are members of groups, often organised ones, of institutions whose existence predates and outlasts the genocidal moment. Some of these organisations do overlap with those organisations and institutions which play an important role in the destruction process – bureaucracies, professional groups of various kinds.

What this suggests is that explanations for bystander behaviour are likely to rest in large part on the kinds of answers that account for perpetrators. Certainly, if there is nothing unusual or disturbed about the ordinary men and women who became perpetrators, then the same must apply *a fortiori* to bystanders. They share and participate in the culture which, to follow Alex Hinton, provides some of the context for particular aspects of a given genocide. They grow up and live within the same framework of beliefs as perpetrators, even if the latter may have distorted and perverted them. If we follow Chirot and McCauley, they are likely to be governed by the same kind of emotions, although fear rather than anger, hate or disgust, for example, is likely to play a greater role for individuals, particularly fear of perpetrators. If we follow the conformity/obedience/peer group pressure/careerism approach, it is not difficult to see how members of institutions that have come to play an important role in the genocide will not wish to be seen as disruptive or disloyal.

Alternatively, to follow the dispositional approach, it can be argued that similar traits may be observed in a milder form. Steven Baum argues, for example, that there are significant differences in mental health between perpetrators at one end and rescuers at the other. The former identify excessively with the group, while the latter are characterised by a much greater autonomy and independent sense of self. Bystanders on his account are somewhere in the middle, and their insufficient sense of autonomy and independence helps explain their indifference.[28]

## Victims

For victims, this indifference is in many ways decisive. By the time genocide is underway, the victims cannot do much to help themselves, although they can sometimes help each other.

Not everyone agrees that victims are always completely powerless or innocent. Perpetrators predictably often claim that the targeted group is a threat (which is why it has to be destroyed) but there are arguments too that rebellion can be a catalyst for genocide (see Chapter 7). This raises questions in turn of course. Is rebellion then not justified if the outcome is genocide? Does this not place the responsibility for genocide on the victim rather than the perpetrator? How do we distinguish between a rebellion which is the catalyst for genocide and resistance against genocide? In any event, genocide is always a grotesquely disproportionate 'response'. Whatever any original 'offence', nothing can justify the destruction of the group itself.

There is no 'guilt' here moreover which would enable one to establish any kind of hierarchy of victims or suffering. Whatever the complexities of the situation, it is the destruction of the group which is the crime. The large numbers (usually) involved make it impossible to make meaningful distinctions about who suffered most; in fact it is demeaning even to want to do so. The experience of destruction for each group is what it is. It demands to be heard and witnessed, not to be 'ranked'.

A fundamental problem for victims is that they find themselves in an asymmetrical situation. They are confronted with a dire and restricted set of choices – to escape, to hide, to delay the process of destruction or physically to fight back, all in circumstances not of their own choosing. It needs to be remembered that for a large proportion of the victim group, many of these choices barely exist at all.

## Gendercide

This is particularly important in the context of what has been called 'gendercide'.[29] Perhaps increasingly, perpetrators seem to be targeting adult men first, clearing the way for sustained campaigns of sexual violence against women. This does not mean that men are not also victims of sexual violence or that women are not also perpetrators. But it is a dimension of the experience of victims that needs emphasising. It is devastating in itself and also because it can be very hard for women even to talk later about what happened, even when the perpetrators have gone. It also has (intended) terrible consequences for the group's ability to reproduce itself.

Even for the minority who are able to consider realistically the option of fighting back, there is a serious problem with information. An important weapon in the genocidal armoury is secrecy, notwithstanding the significance of propaganda and mobilisation. This is one of the elements of denial that Stanton referred to. Perpetrators deny they are going to commit genocide as well as denying that they are doing or have done so. It can then be very difficult for victims often to imagine fully what is being planned for them. Almost all accounts testify to the surprise and confusion in victim groups as they are targeted. Since they do not usually know what is in store for them, it is hard to work out what the best tactics might be.

This can be particularly difficult if there are collaborators within the victim group (see the case of the PACs in Guatemala and the *Jahsh* in Iraq in Chapters 5 and 6). This can be an important weapon of the organisers of genocide. It sows both confusion and demoralisation, adding to the effects of seeing neighbours turning into killers.

The level of demoralisation caused by genocide, with or without collaboration, is always great. For survivors, it raises fundamental questions about how to respond after genocide. How can people return to their homes, often alongside perpetrators and bystanders? Many victims of genocide can end up feeling, quite understandably, that they do not belong any longer in a multi-cultural, multi-ethnic community and that permanent separation is the only answer. It is important to recall that genocide is not only a project of destruction. It is also a project of reconstruction or remaking a national community, as Daniel Feierstein has argued,[30] even if the project is often based on a fantasy about some mythical past when the targeted group were supposedly absent.

One danger for the targeted group is that they can come to believe this too and believe that those targeting them are also 'essentially' different and bad. This perception can generate calls for revenge, which can lead to very violent action and gross human rights violations in turn, as in the case of the Rwandan Patriotic Front's pursuit of Hutus after the genocide (see Chapter 6).

## Rescuers

It may be a lot to ask of survivors, brutalised, traumatised and grieving, not to give in to feelings of revenge or to want to leave the place of genocide forever. One lesson they may draw is that, in the modern world, when other nation states are so reluctant to come to their aid, the safest recourse is to command one's own nation state. The desire of Kurds, like the Jews before them, to be given their own state, for example, given the genocides they have experienced, is entirely understandable. This is not always an option of course. Most victims of genocide have nowhere else to go, no alternative but to try to rebuild their collective life as a group in the place where their families and communities were attacked.

If they are to do so, they will need to hold on to the idea that not everyone is a perpetrator or a bystander, that there have also been rescuers. Relatively little attention has been given to this group, understandably enough, given the gravity and scale of the crime. Nevertheless, there is evidence to suggest that they form a significant part of the population in many cases. As Baum points out, there are quite a large number of what he calls 'defiants' in many of the experiments in social psychology which have otherwise generated quite gloomy conclusions. His close study of three of the classic conformity studies (including the Milgram one) reveals that 'a substantial number of subjects did not conform' and that there are in fact as many potential rescuers as perpetrators (15–20 per cent in each case).[31]

This is a rather striking finding. It raises questions about what can be so special about what seems to be quite a large group. It was thought for some time that rescuers were quite extra-ordinary people and, although they typically seem to deny this themselves there is no doubt that some of them are (and this modesty is part of what makes them so remarkable).[32] It clearly takes considerable courage in many circumstances to go against a determined group of perpetrators and the passivity of bystanders. Why would people take what can be great risks to themselves?

Classic studies of rescuers in the Holocaust have largely concentrated on the beliefs and personality of altruistic individuals.[33] It does not appear to rescuers to matter much whether or not people are of the same nationality, or ethnic group, or religion, let alone 'race'. The values that appear to be shared are fundamentally universalistic and involve a commitment to democracy, to toleration and a belief in social justice. These are not necessarily thought through but, at the moment of decision, it seems that there is a strong sense that here is a fellow human being who just has to be helped.

More recent research, however, suggests that concentrating on the moral psychology of a few clearly outstanding people does not give a full enough picture of the phenomenon of rescue.[34] Locating rescue in the political and historical context of genocide suggests that a number of other factors need to be considered. These can include the scale and speed of the genocide; the proximity of safe places; social and political and local networks; even economic resources. Considering such factors may help illuminate the difficult issue, raised at the beginning of this chapter, of those who could be rescuers one minute and perpetrators at another. The decision to rescue may be a long-lasting commitment but sometimes people can change their minds. Under pressure from the arrival of determined killers, for example, local officials who had been protecting people in Rwanda turned into perpetrators themselves (see Chapter 6). The longer the genocide goes on, the more it undermines solidarity between citizens and the greater the risks rescuers may have to run.

If it is true that rescue is a complex issue and about more than altruistic individuals, it is important nevertheless not to lose sight of the example that they set. Genocide is clearly not inevitable. Even if it has recurred on a very disturbing scale since the Convention, it does not happen always or everywhere, and when it does, people have choices, ordinary people as much as professionals, as much as elites. For all our efforts to explain genocide, it remains at bottom a moral question, a choice between acts, behaviours and paths. How this choice has been exercised in specific genocides is something we turn to in the next two chapters.

# 5    Genocide during the Cold War

The alliance between the United States and the Soviet Union, which had brought an end to the Second World War and so indirectly to the Holocaust, broke up quite quickly. This was to have serious consequences for the international community's will to deal with the problem of genocide.

From 1948 to the collapse of the Soviet Union in 1991, there were several genocides. In this chapter, we look at four cases. Any selection is likely to be arbitrary to some extent but these have been chosen because they exhibit some recurring features, as well as some interesting differences. They show how visions of the nation inform the decision by elites to commit genocide, whether the victims are on the left or the right. They involve varying levels of participation and collaboration, with different kinds of motives. They show how genocide is a global problem – the genocides discussed here took place in Latin America, in the Indian sub-continent and in different parts of Asia.

Africa was not immune, even then. One case discussed in the next chapter (Rwanda) has some roots and antecedents in the genocide in Burundi in this period. The case of Biafra could also have been included here. The assault on the Ibos in the south-east of Nigeria, when they sought to secede, was a compelling example of how one powerful group in control of a post-colonial state could use its sovereign power to attack a weaker one. This case, in which more than a million died, led to the founding of a very important non-governmental organisation, Médecins Sans Frontières (MSF), in part because of frustration with the response of the international community. NGOs such as MSF have come to play an important role in shaping a different response to genocide, helping to develop both a new doctrine, the *Responsibility to Protect*, and an international court, the ICC, to prosecute perpetrators (see Chapters 7 and 8). It was to take several more genocides, however, before such developments could take place.

# Indonesia 1965

## Antecedents and context

One of these genocides took place in Indonesia, in a state which had emerged after the Second World War as part of the anti-colonial struggle, wresting independence from the Dutch. Indonesia is a multi-ethnic and multi-confessional society, although Islam is by far the dominant religion. The national liberation movement was led by Sukarno, who brought together an alliance of forces and ideas in what was known as 'Guided Democracy' or NASAKOM, an amalgam of nationalism, religion and communism. An important role in this alliance was played by the Indonesian Communist Party (the PKI) which took its inspiration from the Communist Party of China. The PKI had become increasingly powerful, particularly as the state of the Indonesian economy deteriorated seriously in the early 1960s. But in 1965 a series of events occurred which were to destroy the party, involving an explosion of state-sponsored violence against large numbers of unarmed Indonesian citizens.

The precise details of what happened are still not entirely clear. Some communists, reporting to the Communist Party leader D. N. Aidit but probably not with the knowledge or approval of other party leaders, arrested a number of generals. Whether this was to pre-empt what in fact then happened to the party or was even a full-blown coup is not certain. Several generals were killed but one, Suharto, was not arrested, for reasons which remain obscure; it is possible that he was even privy to the plot. Suharto then organised the crushing of what he presented as a sinister, evil and alien conspiracy against the Indonesian nation.

## Victims

### An account of the killing in Indonesia

Pak Karto and Pak Ismail were members of Communist organisations before 1965. Both fled their homes and went on the run when the anti-Communist violence began shortly after the 1 October coup.

'Night and day we ran and hid. We hid in the forest. We ran for a long, long time. During the day we would sleep in the forest, taking it in turns to be on watch, taking it in turns to sleep. When we ran out of food, if we were brave enough, we'd go to a village, hungry, and ask for some food. If we heard the mob coming, we'd run and hide again. Soldiers were hunting us, and mobs who had spears, sticks, machetes, bamboo spears. If you were spotted, they would attack immediately.'

'In this area, the mob was a mix of people. There were lots of soldiers. The vigilante mobs around here were on a mission to catch us, and there were other groups too who had gotten together, gotten together to hunt us down. They considered us people who were fit to be killed the moment we were hunted down. We had our throats cut and were thrown into the river.'

After a few months of being on the run, Pak Karto and Pak Ismail were captured and taken to a detention camp that had been set up by the local military. There they were interrogated and tortured, starved, humiliated and forced to live in over-crowded, squalid conditions with hundreds of other detainees.

'We were in detention together. Our experiences there were very bitter for us. They beat us with a goal in mind, to try to make us confess to something. No-one would confess to anything. The officer would be mad at us for not answering. He'd ask a question, and we'd just sit there, so he'd grab a stick and start beating us. This went on for days. We would have to take our clothes off and were forced to bake in the sun. For days it went on like that. We were beaten for no reason, only that they'd been told to beat us. If we didn't answer, they'd beat us too. Every few hours, we were processed (interrogated). At three o'clock in the morning! I was processed, electrocuted, beaten. Other people were taken away in the night and didn't come back again. "Borrowed", taken away ... but they were executed.'

(From a transcript of an interview conducted by Annie Pohlman with Pak Karto and Pak Ismail, West Sumatra, September 2005.)

The primary victims of the genocide were those identified as communists, although this was a quite elastic label, especially at the local level. Large numbers of supposed communists and their allies were hunted down, arrested, tortured and executed in a period lasting from October 1965 to approximately March 1966, although the killings and deaths continued for some time after that. The precise numbers have never been agreed, with estimates ranging from 500,000 to 1,000,000 or even more. Unlike some other perpetrators, the Indonesian state did not keep records of what happened at the time.

The violence took place across Indonesia as a whole, although with some significant local variations. It was particularly bloody in Java and

Bali. Robert Cribb, probably the leading expert on the genocide, has identified two distinct patterns.[1] One involved a hunt of communists from house to house and village to village, with killings mostly taking place at night by machete. This was followed by the torture and killing of the large number of 'suspects' rounded up and detained in various prisons or camps. Alongside the killing, which also involved dismemberment of bodies, and even in some cases drinking the blood of victims, there was very considerable sexual violence against women. It was a traumatic experience for the whole of society which has left its mark to this day.

*Perpetrators*

At the head of the elite who organised the genocide were General Suharto and his fellow generals. The main perpetrator was the Indonesian army they commanded. Elite units of the army conducted the military operations in Central and Western Java, where much of the killing took place. However, the army did not act alone. There were also local militias, mobilised by the army, who did much of the killing, particularly in Eastern Java and Bali. There was also extensive local involvement which went beyond these militias.

Anthropologists have emphasised the significance of local grudges and scores being settled in villages where communist membership, affiliation or sympathy is not so easy to discern. Many victims protested that they had nothing to do with communism at all. This was not disingenuous. It appears that conflicts over land, economic inequality, wealth, status and inheritance played an important part in the violence. Of course the PKI was itself involved in many of these conflicts already, as it had established support and networks in towns and villages across the country. However, it still seems that material motivations were probably more important than ideological animus at the local level.[2]

For the military elite, on the other hand, anti-communism was certainly the key factor. It was too for their allies, the political and religious conservatives and social and economic elites, all of whom saw the communists as a threat. It was their collective anti-communism which, in the epoch of the Cold War, attracted the support and encouragement of the United States, which furnished extensive lists of communists for Suharto to arrest.

At the local level though, cultural systems and codes did play an important role. They enabled people to make their own sense of the violence they were now being permitted and encouraged to act out or watch unfold. A particular Balinese sense of social uncertainty, for example, helped to create a general feeling that violence was somehow inevitable. Some of this anxiety even seems to have had a supernatural expression, with communists being identified as *leaks,* beings with demonic powers capable of changing shape which had to be unmasked.[3] There was also a paralysing fear of the power of local 'tough guys' (*jagos*), which may account for some of the victims' apparent passivity.[4]

## *Intent*

On the other hand, the lack of resistance attests to the great imbalance between perpetrators and victims, and the one-sided character of this genocide. It was implemented quite swiftly and well co-ordinated by the central state, whilst those targeted for destruction had few resources to counter the assault waged upon them.

It can be argued, of course, that what happened in this case was actually not genocide, as the target was the Communist Party, and political groups are not included in the Convention. It was thought at one time that it was still genocide, because many of those killed were Chinese. But it has subsequently been estimated that no more than 2,000 out of a population of about 2,500,000 Chinese were killed. Few Chinese were involved with the PKI, despite its close ties with the Chinese communists, and few were living in the areas where the killing took place. In fact, it can be argued that the assumption that the killing was aimed at Chinese is itself a form of denial, obscuring the real target and how and why they were selected.[5]

Rather than the Chinese, it was communists, as Cribb has argued, who were constructed as enemies of the nation.[6] The genocide was intended to reconstruct the Indonesian nation itself. It was not sufficient just to kill, torture and detain communists at the time. The 'taint' of communism hung too over subsequent generations who had to be permanently watched over and were systematically marginalised. The genocide was followed by the 'New Order' and the creation of a so-called 'clean environment'. Employment and promotion within the state or key sectors of the economy could only be achieved with a certificate attesting to the absence of any previous communist association. This applied not only to those suspected of involvement at the time but also their children. Political identity, it turned out, was not something that was chosen, a belief or commitment that could be renounced. It was attributed and projected – not just to those killed but also to their descendants, guilty by birth, by connection, by proximity.

## Rescue, intervention, aftermath

There was no rescue from this genocide, from within or without. It came to an end only when the perpetrators had had enough. As long as they remained in power, there was no questioning of what had happened inside Indonesia. There was little questioning outside too. In the epoch of the Cold War, the US government was extremely satisfied with the elimination of a communist threat in the region. None of its Western allies raised the question but neither too did their antagonists. China did not want attention drawn to the unpreparedness of its loyal followers, since uncomfortable questions might then have been asked about its own advice and leadership. The victims were abandoned on all sides.

What is perhaps even more striking is the lack of interest in this case even today, from within or without. Even when the perpetrators went on to commit genocide again, as they did in East Timor (see Chapter 7), there has been little call for a sustained investigation. There has been no real effort to establish the truth or to accord justice to the victims. It could be argued that this is because the ideology that was at issue here, communism, has now effectively disappeared from the historical stage. Who could now be interested in an injustice meted out to those who followed what has turned out to be a bankrupt ideology and one guilty of its own genocidal crimes? But this is not wholly persuasive, not least because 'communism' was such an elastic category at the local level. It seems more plausible to attribute the lack of interest here to widespread collusion, collaboration and bystanding, to the material and emotional motives which enabled and justified the killing in the first place.

This is an alarming thought. It suggests that if enough people in a society can be brought by the state to participate and benefit in genocide, and if the violence can be successfully implemented against a group lacking any support or sympathy from without, the perpetrators may benefit from impunity for good. Even worse, it means that the genocidal state remains intact and could strike again, as indeed it did (see Chapter 7).

## Bangladesh 1971

### Antecedents and context

Some five years after the Indonesian killings had been concluded, genocide occurred again, this time in East Pakistan. Again, it was a genocide committed by a recently created post-colonial state. Here however, the state was the product of a division, the Partition of India in 1947, itself a very bloody affair, displacing some 12.5 million people and leaving up to 1 million dead.

The two parts of Pakistan were separated by over 1,000 miles but the separation was more than physical. Although Pakistan had been created as a Muslim state, East Pakistan was home in fact to some 10–12 million Hindus, who formed 13 per cent of the population. They lived alongside their Muslim fellow Bengali-speaking citizens. Together they formed a majority of the population of Pakistan as a whole but experienced significant and growing inequalities and discrimination. Per capita income in West Pakistan for example, which was 32 per cent higher than East Pakistan in 1960, was 61 per cent higher by the end of the decade.[7] Political inequalities accompanied these disparities in wealth, with power largely concentrated in the hands of an elite in the West.

After a coup in 1958, the country was governed by the army who retained a tight grip for over a decade, first under Ayub Khan and then Yahya Khan, before agreeing under pressure to oversee a transition to democracy at the end of the 1960s. In 1970, however, there was a terrible cyclone which led to half a million deaths in East Pakistan. This was handled poorly by the authorities, creating a renewed focus for discontent. Elections that year had produced a stunning victory in East Pakistan for the Awami League, which had campaigned for greater autonomy. They won 167 out of 169 possible seats. Their demands were unacceptable to the military and also to political parties in West Pakistan, who viewed the League as a major threat to the unity and integrity of the nation. After abortive and probably not serious negotiations, Yahya Khan took the decision to suppress what had until then been largely non-violent protest.

## Victims

### An account of the killing in Bangladesh

In the dead region surrounding Dacca, the military authorities conducted experiments in mass extermination in places unlikely to be seen by journalists. At Hariharpara, a once thriving village on the banks of the Buriganga River near Dacca, they found the three elements necessary for killing people in large numbers: a prison in which to hold the victims, a place for executing the prisoners and a method for disposing of the bodies. The prison was a large riverside warehouse, or godown, belonging to the

Pakistan National Oil Company, the place of execution was the river edge, or the shallows near the shore, and the bodies were disposed of by the simple means of permitting them to float downstream. The killing took place night after night. Usually the prisoners were roped together and made to wade out into the river. They were in batches of six or eight, and in the light of a powerful electric arc lamp, they were easy targets, black against the silvery water. The executioners stood on the pier, shooting down at the compact bunches of prisoners wading in the water. There were screams in the hot night air, and then silence. The prisoners fell on their sides and their bodies lapped against the shore. Then a new bunch of prisoners was brought out, and the process was repeated. In the morning the village boatmen hauled the bodies into midstream and the ropes binding the bodies were cut so that each body drifted separately downstream.

(From Stephen Pierre and Robert Payne, *Massacre*, Basingstoke: Macmillan, 1973, p.55; cited in http://www.genocide-bangladesh.org)

The genocide began with a ferocious assault ('Operation Searchlight') on the capital of East Pakistan, Dhaka, spreading out to other towns and villages across the region. It has been claimed that the generals were prepared to kill up to 4 million people to crush the movement and the general in charge of the Dhaka operation talked about a 'Final Solution'. Far from being cowed, however, the movement declared independence.

Precisely in order to avoid such an outcome, the perpetrators of the genocide had targeted specific groups of civilians to begin with – intellectuals and students and leaders and members of the Awami League, along with sections of the local state deemed to be unreliable, including the police. Although the killings had a religious dimension, aiming to eliminate the Hindu population of East Pakistan, the majority of the victims were actually ordinary Muslims. Given that Pakistan was created as a Muslim state, this is particularly striking. It has been described as 'probably the only modern genocide in which a so-called Islamic republic set out to kill Muslims, even though Hindus and other minorities were also targeted'.[8]

Estimates vary of how many were killed, somewhere between 1 million and 3 million, but huge numbers of people were also displaced. Some 10 million refugees (the large majority of them Hindus) fled to India, including about a quarter of the population of Dhaka. Along with the killing went extreme sexual violence. It is estimated that somewhere between 200,000 and 400,000 women were raped, some of them repeatedly, many of them as captives in military camps, others in front of their families.

This initial violence was not used against rebels but against civilians. It was then followed by an armed rebellion, a guerrilla war waged by those now fighting for national liberation from Pakistan (the *Mukta Bahini*), but this was in response to the genocide not a cause of it. It is true that the guerrillas were supported by the Indian army and that there was then a war between Pakistan and India, triggered by an attack by Pakistan. In the course of that conflict, there was considerable further violence, much of it retributive against collaborators, but however appalling, it was not itself genocidal.

## Perpetrators

The primary perpetrators were the generals of the army, Yahya Khan and his associates, none of whom were ever brought to justice for their crimes. Several agencies and groups were mobilised by the army for the genocide, both political groups (such as the *Jamaat-e-Islam*) but also auxiliaries, particularly a force known as the *Razakars*. This was made up of police and 'rangers' brought over from West Pakistan but also included local collaborators who were a mix of fundamentalist Muslims, criminals and armed robbers (*dacoity*). Some were Bengali but many were Biharis, mostly Urdu-speaking Muslims who had migrated to East Pakistan. It has been suggested that some of the violence was due to officers and soldiers and collaborators getting out of control but clearly immense violence was intended from the outset.[9]

## Intent

There was a general reluctance to see this as genocide from the outset. The US government, for whom Pakistan was an important ally, suppressed internal reports at the time claiming that it was genocide. However, many critics of the United States have also shown remarkably little interest in this case, perhaps because the United States did not play a sufficiently prominent role or because the leaders of the resistance were not politically congenial.[10]

The retributive violence that followed from the resistance and the outcome may also have made it easier to cast it as a secessionist conflict. It is true that the motive of the military elite (supported by politicians in West Pakistan) was, on the face of it, to preserve the territorial integrity of Pakistan. The violence certainly escalated, from the killing of many non-combatant civilians to the destruction of whole villages, a wave of executions and mass rape. As the resistance movement developed, there was certainly violence too from that quarter but this was met by even further, more extreme violence from the army and its collaborators. The focus of destruction, however, were those clearly regarded as not part of the nation – not just Hindus but also, and in larger numbers, disloyal Muslims. They were seen as different and inferior, too soft, too tolerant, too secular in comparison to those in West Pakistan. Yahya Khan's predecessor had even claimed that East Bengalis probably belonged to 'original Indian races' and had long been dominated by 'Hindu cultural and linguistic influence'.

The only remedy, in the eyes of the perpetrators, was the eradication of alien and suspect elements. A senior army commander called it 'a war between the pure and the impure. The people here may have Muslim names and call themselves Muslims. But they are Hindu at heart. We are now sorting them out ... Those who are left will be real Muslims'.[11] The intent was to destroy not just the substantial Hindu population but many others too, to reconstruct a purer Pakistan that would be more homogeneous, more faithfully Muslim and more loyal.

### Rescue, intervention, aftermath

This aim was thwarted by the resistance but also, more decisively, by India. As the refugees fled into India, creating a major humanitarian crisis, India appealed to the United Nations to take action. But as Nicholas Wheeler has shown, 'in the face of mass killing in East Pakistan, the overwhelming reaction of the society of states was to affirm Pakistan's right to sovereignty'.[12] The first to rush to support Pakistan were non-Arab Muslim states. Both the United States and China adopted this position too. The United States viewed India as a Soviet ally, but so too did China, to whom it was now reaching out. China also feared any precedent that would weaken the principle of national sovereignty, with any implications for what was going on within its own borders. There had been immense violence in the 1960s in the Cultural Revolution, and millions more had died in the so-called Great Leap Forward, an economic policy which had led to mass starvation, on an even worse scale than the Ukrainian genocide caused by Stalin in the 1930s.

By now India was not only assisting the refugees as best it could but also providing support to the resistance. Although it did not formally recognise Bangladesh initially, it did so as war with Pakistan broke out. The war ended in defeat for Pakistan, and the Indian army was therefore able to bring the genocide to an end. No other force could have done so. The resistance, although effective enough as a guerrilla movement, could not stop it. Faced with widespread international criticism, however, India itself backtracked on the argument that it was intervening to stop genocide. Instead it had recourse to the (evidently more acceptable) argument that it was acting in self-defence, that its own territorial integrity had been breached by the attack from Pakistan. This was true enough but scarcely the main point.

The fact that genocide had taken place was then largely obscured, even within Bangladesh itself. Considerable political instability followed independence, making it difficult to address what had happened. Indeed the leader of the resistance and first President of Bangladesh, Sheikh Mujibur Rahman, was assassinated in 1975. The main focus was initially on collaborators inside what had been East Pakistan rather than on the primary perpetrators, who were of course in West Pakistan. There was an enquiry there, not into the genocide but why the war and East Pakistan had been lost. In Bangladesh itself, a Collaborators (Special Tribunal) Order was issued in 1972 and an International Crimes (Tribunal) Act was drafted in 1973. This was not however pursued with much vigour. It was amended in 2009 but has, in the eyes of jurists, several key weaknesses, to do with due process, the death penalty and the possibility of a fair trial.[13] On the part of the international community, however, there has been complete inaction: the genocide, denied at the time, has largely disappeared from view.

## Cambodia 1975–9

### *Antecedents and context*

Only four years later, there was an even more violent genocide in Cambodia. Unlike Pakistan, Cambodia was not an entirely new state, but had regained its independence in the context of decolonisation, from the French. There was some history of previous genocidal episodes, with large-scale massacres of the Vietnamese in the seventeenth and eighteenth centuries. This past antagonism did cast some shadow over what was to happen in the 1970s.[14] Of more immediate significance, however, was the impact of the Vietnam War. From 1969 to 1973, seeking to disrupt North Vietnam's supply lines, the United States dropped dropped nearly three times as many bombs on Cambodia as had been dropped on Japan in World War II.[15] At the same time, the United States had backed the removal of Prince Sihanouk, the ruler of Cambodia. He was replaced by General Lon Nol, whose corrupt and authoritarian rule was deeply unpopular. As the Americans were defeated in Vietnam and support for Lon Nol withdrawn, an insurgency led by the Cambodian Communist Party swept him from power, taking the capital Phnom Penh on 17 April 1975.

The Cambodian Communist Party had originally been part of a larger Indochinese Communist Party, but had formed a separate organisation in 1951. After much factional infighting, a tight-knit, highly secretive leadership had taken over. Its core was composed of intellectuals educated in Paris. Here they had developed a syncretic ideology, a toxic mix of anti-colonial, nationalist, racist, Stalinist and Maoist ideas. All members of the party were required to give the leadership unquestioning and total obedience. They became known as the Khmer Rouge – the Khmer being the largest ethnic group in Cambodia. The Khmer Empire had dominated the region between the ninth and thirteenth century, a period the party leaders looked back to for some inspiration. The name of its capital, Angkor, was adopted by the Party's central committee which was called *Angkor Loeu* – the 'high organisation'.

*Victims*

## A survivor's account of the Cambodian genocide

On April 17, 1975, when I was fourteen years old, the Khmer Rouge army came into Phnom Penh with tanks. ... Soldiers came to our house with their guns and ordered us to leave.

... These soldiers were our countrymen. We had no reason not to believe them. They weren't going to let us get hurt.

... We walked for days, then weeks. Pregnant women gave birth under trees by the road. Old people died from exhaustion and lack of water. Everywhere was the sound of babies screaming and people crying for loved ones who had died and had to be left on the road.

... There was no time for funerals. Soldiers threw the bodies into empty ponds and kept everyone moving. Guns were pointed at us, and tanks forced us to keep moving. I saw two men with their hands tied behind their backs. Soldiers were questioning them on the side of the road. The soldiers cut off the men's heads, which fell to the ground as their bodies slumped. There was nothing I could do. People were being murdered before my eyes.

... Finally after almost two and a half months of walking and stopping, we arrived outside the province of Battambong, where most of the villages had burned to ashes during the fighting. We were told that we must live in these burned-out villages.

... All of us started to get sick from malnutrition. There was no medicine and no doctors ... My sister's ten-year-old son got diarrhoea and died after three days of suffering. My sister went crazy with grief. She would not move from the spot where we buried them. She never recovered.

... After we had been in our hut for about a year, the soldiers came to take my grandfather.

... Three months after my grandfather was murdered, the soldiers took my brother and brother in law.

... Within about three months, after the deaths of my aunts, my grandmother died, and then my older sister.

... Soon after that my mother died. I wanted to die too. She had always taken care of me and I had depended on her. Now there was no one to take care of me. Soon my little brother died ... Now only my sister and I remained.

It was my responsibility as the oldest male to protect my sister. My mother would be counting on me. But there was nothing I could do. And one day, as we sat together in the hut, Sinuoen put her head on my lap and said 'Kimny, I don't know if I can live any longer. Can I have a spoon of rice?'

My heart was breaking. It was such a little thing she asked. But I had no rice.

(From Youkimny Chan, 'One Spoon of Rice' in *Children of Cambodia's Killing Fields – Memories by Survivors,* compiled by Dith Pran, New Haven, CT: Yale University Press, pp.2–24.)

There had in fact already been significant violence both in eliminating internal rivals and in areas the Khmer Rouge had controlled prior to victory. It was though but a prelude to what was now to happen to the largely unsuspecting, diverse and multi-ethnic population of Cambodia.

The Khmer Rouge's first step was to evacuate Phnom Penh itself, supposedly to protect the population from further American bombing. The large urban population was marched off to the countryside. Here they were forced to work for the peasants, now glorified as 'old' people (in contrast to the supposedly 'new' people from the cities). The Khmer Rouge stirred up peasant animosity towards the displaced urban population, invoking past humiliations, oppression and 'class' exploitation. The deported urban population was now condemned to forced labour, to work and live in appalling conditions that soon turned into widespread famine and starvation. This was entirely foreseeable. Not only did they have no experience or training to work on the land but agriculture had already been devastated by American bombing.

But death from overwork and lack of food was only one part of the horror that was unfolding. From the beginning, there were mass executions of purported enemies of the people, which included those suspected even inside the Party of disloyalty to the leaders. The violence inflicted was brutal, involving torture, rape and even cannibalism.

The victims came from every quarter of Cambodian society but with a particular hatred directed at certain groups. Anyone with an education was suspect, as were those with foreign contacts of any kind. One third of all city dwellers died, but so too did 15 per cent of the rural population. Members of religious groups were also targeted. It has been estimated that fewer than 2,000 of Cambodia's 70,000 Buddhist monks were alive when the genocide was over.[16] But perhaps the most directly targeted of all were ethnic minorities. Almost the entire Vietnamese population (20,000 people) of Cambodia was wiped out, along with half of the Chinese (215,000) and around a third of the Cham (90,000), of the Thai (8,000) and the Lao (4,000). The overall figures were stunning – around 1.7 million out of a total population of about 8 million.[17]

## Perpetrators

The primary perpetrators of this genocide were the central leadership of the party – Pol Pot, Nuon Chea, Khieu Samphan, Ieng Sary and Son Sen. They formed a highly secretive group. Pol Pot (whose real name was Saloth Sar) gave himself the ostensibly egalitarian moniker 'Brother Number One'. He was not in fact a worker or a peasant but a child of a moderately wealthy family with some connections to the court, educated in a royal monastery and an elite Catholic school. His closest associates were also not workers or poor peasants.

This elite exercised a tight grip on the Communist Party, effectively merging it with the state. The latter was in many ways quite undeveloped, particularly after the devastation wrought by war, so there was no extensive bureaucracy involved in planning and implementing the genocide. The central role was played rather by the dreaded security forces (*santesok*), reporting to the elite and bypassing the formal party structure and regional party leaders, many of whom were themselves to be arrested, imprisoned and murdered.

One particular facility was a terrifying prison, known as S-21 at Tuol Sleng, directed by a man known as Deuch, where 20,000 were detained, tortured and murdered in a closely monitored process, with detailed records kept of what was done, to whom and (supposedly) why. In what has been described as a 'total institution', there was a carefully worked out division of labour between interrogators, those in charge of documentation and a whole set of sub-units with 'capturers', motorised sections, economic 'support units', even excrement bearers.[18] Many of the younger low-level subordinates were middle peasants, removed from their families and communities. The division of labour also fostered an atomisation among the guards that left them particularly vulnerable to indoctrination, especially given their lack of education.

Alex Hinton has argued nevertheless that this cannot be understood as a simple top-down process. Perpetrators were motivated by fear and anxiety that they too would be punished if they did not play their role faithfully and effectively, but they also gained some sense of self-worth through humiliating and inflicting violence on their victims.[19] Moreover the regime was able to draw on local cultural norms to mobilise violence. Performances, songs and dance were all used to arouse the suppressed hatred of peasants towards city dwellers, inflaming grudges, and evoking a thirst for revenge.[20]

## Intent

Like Stalin and Mao, only even more so, Pol Pot believed that political will and ruthless violence could lead to the creation of a new society. The year the Khmer Rouge came to power was declared 'Year Zero'. The social base of this society would be the peasants. The entire society was subjected to a radical, utopian experiment. Cambodia was to become entirely self-sufficient, with a collectivised agricultural economy directed by the all-seeing, omniscient leadership of the *Angkar*.

As this project ran into inevitable problems, Pol Pot and his associates became increasingly paranoid, seeing enemies everywhere. Sometimes these were described in class terms but ethnic groups were seen as even more dangerous, especially the Vietnamese. There was a pseudo-medical obsession with 'sickness' and 'illness' and with 'microbes' which had to be entirely eradicated, because (according to Pol Pot) even 'if we scratch the ground to bury them, they will rot us from within'.[21] Cambodia was likened to a garden which had to be weeded ('to dig up grass, one must also dig up the roots') or to a body which had to be cleaned and purified.[22]

The only possible objection to categorising this as genocide is that it was inflicted on the same group as the one to which the perpetrators belonged, the Khmer. But leaving aside the fact that many others were also killed, 'auto-genocide' as it is sometimes called is not excluded by the Convention. This genocide too resulted from an effort to reimagine and refashion the national community. To implement that vision, many people had to suffer famine, starvation and super-exploitation and many had to be directly eliminated – those who disagreed, those suspected of disloyalty, those from the wrong 'class', those who were not Khmer – a very large number indeed.

### Rescue, intervention, aftermath

The corollary again was that, faced with the overwhelming power of the state, rescue could only come from without. The genocide only ended when the Vietnamese invaded and overthrew the Khmer Rouge. The Vietnamese had of course been the object of genocidal attacks inside Cambodia (Pol Pot's policy was to kill 30 Vietnamese for every Khmer) but Vietnam itself had also been attacked. Many Cambodians, including former members of the Khmer Rouge, had fled there, and it was these people the Vietnamese now placed in power in Phnom Penh.

There are several paradoxes with this outcome. One is that the Vietnamese had helped develop the Cambodian Communist Party in the first place, before Pol Pot revealed himself to be a racist xenophobe. Another is the reason Vietnam gave for intervening, which was supposedly to secure its own borders. Unlike India, the Vietnamese did not even try to invoke the humanitarian issue, even though only their intervention halted the genocide.

Nevertheless, the United States and most of the international community now denounced Vietnam for its intervention, refusing to recognise the new government. Even if Pol Pot was a communist, he was an enemy of the Vietnamese, and 'objectively' a potential ally. It might be thought that critics of the United States would have attacked it for this. In fact, many turned a blind eye or worse, in some cases suggesting that reports of genocide were being vastly exaggerated, as part of a continuing anti-communist hysteria.[23] They were not alone in fostering a climate of denial. China too actually sponsored the UN resolution condemning Vietnam's 'aggression'. A number of liberal democracies like Norway, Australia and New Zealand, as well as non-aligned states, lined up to criticise Vietnam. Only the Soviet bloc supported Vietnam but as self-defence, not on the basis of the Convention.[24]

Even if the Vietnamese had managed to end the genocide, however, there was to be no justice. Internally, the new rulers had much blood on their own hands as former members of the Khmer Rouge, and would not investigate or prosecute, for fear their own crimes would come out. Externally, the international community showed little interest. It was not until 2003 (almost 30 years after the genocide) that a tribunal was finally set up, under the mixed auspices of the Cambodians and the UN. It began work in 2006 and the first trial took place in 2009.

Leaving aside the inherent difficulties of such a mixed tribunal, the fact remains that many of the perpetrators had long escaped any kind of justice. To add insult to injury, the main accused (Deuch) contrived both to say that he was deeply remorseful and then to argue that he had only been following orders, before asking for an acquittal! At the time of writing, further trials are to be held of, amongst others, Nuon Chea ('Brother Number Two'), Khieu Samphan and Ieng Sary, but what kind of justice will be implemented and what it can mean to survivors or the people of Cambodia is unclear.

## Guatemala 1981–3

### Antecedents and context

As in Indonesia, the genocide in Guatemala occurred with the collusion and support of the United States. The violence inflicted on a large section of the population of Guatemala by the military in the 1980s took place in a context structured by centuries of colonial exploitation and the strategic priorities of the dominant continental power, the United States. On the one hand there were profound inequalities, between rich and poor, and especially between *ladinos* and the indigenous Mayan populations (there are more than 20 different language groups). On the other hand, there was the US National Security Doctrine which enlisted and trained military rulers across Latin America in a co-ordinated struggle to eliminate any threat from the left, particularly after what was seen as the disaster of the Cuban Revolution in 1959.[25]

In Guatemala, the threat took the form of a leftist guerrilla movement which began to develop in the 1960s. This followed the rolling-back of the limited progressive gains made by the governments of first Arevalo and then Arbenz, who was ousted in a coup engineered by the United States in 1954. The factionalised guerrilla movement achieved little until it adopted a mass-based strategy, mobilising Mayans for the first time. Mayans had for a long time been both heavily exploited and regarded with racist contempt by established *ladino* elites. In the 1960s and 1970s, Mayans were even further marginalised and impoverished by natural disasters (a major earthquake had devastated the country in 1967) and economic crises. By 1982 the new guerrilla strategy was beginning to reap reward and the now united movement had taken control of 9 out of 21 provinces. However, the violent response that it was met with was out of all proportion to the threat posed.

The Guatemalan elite were not alone in Latin America in engaging in genocidal violence against its own population. Argentina, it has been argued, was in some ways the paradigm.[26] A whole raft of techniques were developed there, including the use of concentration camps, the use of terror against the whole society, forced disappearances (abduction, torture and hidden murder) and the removal of children from families. Many of these were taken up elsewhere in the region. It was in Guatemala, however, that the killing was most extensive and the violence most brutal. This violence, for all the influence undoubtedly exercised by the United States, was nevertheless decided upon and committed by the Guatemalan elite.

*Victims*

## A survivor's account of the killings in Guatemala

On August 18, 1982, the soldiers came to organise civilian patrols in the village of Akjel, in the municipality of San Ildefonso Ixtahuacan. They ordered the assistant mayor to convene the people. When people arrived, the second lieutenant began talking, saying that by order of the Efrain Rios Montt government, they were going to organise the civilian patrols.

... 'If you do not want to patrol, then you are subversives. You are going to respect the law, because it comes from the government. And if you don't respect the law that I have announced to you, I will kill your entire village.'

... [In] the village of La Cubre Papal ... the soldiers removed a man named Juan Ordonez from his house, and another neighbour, and they set both of their houses on fire. The houses were made of straw. As the houses were burning, they threw both men, who were tied up very tightly, into the fire. And then they took me down farther, and we ran into two children who were eating corn on the cob in their homes. One ran off and hid ... and the other, a five year-old, stayed inside the house. The soldiers set the house on fire, and burned it down with the child inside ... The soldiers then began to burn the other houses in the village. I could not count them all. I counted at least 20 houses that were burned by the soldiers. Then they let me return to my home.

In the month of November, a white pickup truck arrived. When it came to the Sevillaj bridge near the Cuilco mound, it stopped in front of Sr. José Lopez's house. Soldiers from the truck set his house on fire and then they machined-gunned Sr. Lopez, who was 60 years old, and all his family. They killed a total of 10 people in that house. There was not one single person from José Lopez's family left. Then they forced the civilian patrols, who were accompanying the soldiers, to bury the dead in 6-foot ditches.

(From Susanne Jonas, Ed McCaughan and Elizabeth Sunderland Martinéz (eds), *Guatemala: Tyranny on Trial – Testimony of the Permanent People's Tribunal,* San Francisco: Synthesis Publications, 1984, pp.104–6.)

The primary victims were Mayan, who constituted some 83 per cent of those murdered. The overall death toll was around a quarter of a million out of a total population of 8 million, with around 150,000 unarmed, largely Mayan civilians murdered in two years as the violence (which had been going on already for nearly two decades) was deliberately escalated by the Guatemalan army to a genocidal level. The process of destruction again involved more than mass killings. Whole villages were burnt down in a 'scorched earth' policy – 626 in total. Many inhabitants were 'relocated' to what the army called 'model villages', located in so-called 'development poles', in fact concentration camps.[27] About 1.5 million people were displaced, with over 200,000 fleeing to Mexico, and many dying in the mountains. The destruction of villages was part of a policy of making whole areas unusable for the guerrillas, but also uninhabitable, in a systematic campaign to destroy the infrastructure of independent indigenous life. Crops were burnt and even sacred sites vandalised.

Most of those murdered to start with were men but large numbers of women were also killed – at one point (in mid-1982) indeed more women were being killed than men.[28] Murder was accompanied by rape and torture. The elderly and children were also targets, children not only being parted from their parents but being brutally assaulted. There was also widespread mutilation of bodies. The effect of this violence was traumatic and long-standing, particularly for women who had experienced or witnessed torture, rape and murder at the hands of perpetrators who lived with complete impunity after they had 'triumphed' in their 'war against subversion'. It destroyed deeply rooted communities, transforming established patterns of life, replacing them with one imposed by the perpetrators.

It also sowed deep divisions within Mayan communities, as a significant number of collaborators were enlisted from within to form what were called 'civilian self-defence patrols' (PACs). A large numbers of Mayans were also conscripted for the army (80 per cent of the rank and file were of Mayan descent). Those who refused to turn on their fellow villagers were treated as subversives themselves and killed or sent to the camps. Those who participated in the killing experienced great shame and guilt for what they had been forced to do to their fellow citizens.

*Perpetrators*

The primary perpetrators were the top army generals (all trained in the United States) who decided to wipe out what they called *la subversion* once and for all. In 2008, the key individuals concerned were charged by a Spanish court. They included General Efraim Rios Montt, who took power in a military coup in 1982 and ruled until he too was removed in a coup by General Oscar Humberto Mejia Victores, who was also charged; their predecessor General Fernando Romeo Lucas Garcia (president from 1978 to 1982); and his brother General Benedicto Lucas Garcia (chief of staff in that period).

The charges followed the findings of a remarkable internal Guatemalan Commission for Historical Clarification (CEH) which conducted detailed research into *la violencia*. It found that the army was responsible for 93 per cent of all the human rights violations committed in that period and the guerrillas for only 3 per cent; the remaining 4 per cent could not be attributed with any certainty. The violence was centrally organised and well co-ordinated, with daily intelligence briefings at the highest level, particularly in the implementation of the *Plan Victoria*, described by one general as 'a complete job with planning down to the last detail'.[29]

The army alone, however, was not deemed sufficient to carry out genocide. Alongside it, the generals created the PACs, which by 1984 had enrolled about 900,000 men who were responsible for nearly 20 per cent of the murders. The PACs forcibly recruited about one eighth of the entire population and a quarter of the adult population. They were part of a militarised control structure which reached right down to the local level. The PACs were crucial collaborators, systematically socialised and terrified into committing violence against their fellow citizens, as the army radically polarised Guatemalan society. Rios Montt declared that, 'whoever is against the ... government, whoever doesn't surrender, I'm going to shoot'.[30] In village after village, the army forced Mayans to enlist and to show that they were prepared to kill, torture and rape, or they would be treated as subversives themselves.

*Intent*

This polarisation was a consequence of an ideology which was rooted in a series of binary constructions. Anti-communism was a central element but the enemy was constructed as all that was opposed to a racialised conception of the nation, anchored in a fantasy about its essential place in a supposedly Christian West. This was more than counter-insurgency. It was a determined effort to restructure the nation from above, to create a stronger and more cohesive sense of national identity, imposing a new pattern on Guatemalan society.

The immense human rights violations were identified as 'acts of genocide' rather than a policy of genocide by the CEH. It is clear nevertheless that they flowed directly from an overarching strategy designed to 'drain the sea' in which the guerrillas swam, 'taking the water away from the fish', as Rios Montt put it. The destruction and murder was therefore aimed not just at the guerrillas but at whole communities, which were overwhelmingly Mayan. Guilt was imputed on the basis of ethnic identity to people who had always been regarded as inferior and potentially dangerous, more seriously than ever when they linked up with the guerrillas.

*Rescue, intervention, aftermath*

It took some considerable time before this genocide could be openly discussed at all, such was the persisting climate of fear in Guatemala, even when the killing had been brought to an end. There was again no outside intervention to halt genocide in this case. The United States under President Carter did belatedly object to what the generals were doing but they ignored him completely, carrying on killing even when American aid was halted for a while. Carter's successor, Reagan, then restored links and even defended what the army had been doing. In the epoch of the Cold War, despite their purported anti-imperialist stances, neither the Soviet Union nor China made any protests.

The genocide came to an end only when the killers had had enough. However, they found that they could not establish a stable effective mode of rule, having alienated large sections even of *ladino* civil society. Protracted negotiations eventually took place and resulted in the setting up of the CEH.

Its findings were dramatic and were immediately rejected by the Guatemalan government, which was clearly quite unprepared for such a damning verdict. In a desperate and wholly unconvincing response, the government tried to argue that it was not genocide. It claimed that the violence was 'just' the result of a necessary counter-insurgency against a real threat from the left, that no ethnic group was targeted as such and Mayans were killed only because they joined the insurgency and that Mayans were also perpetrators.

It is revealing that this response tried to enlist the narrowest interpretation of the Convention for the purposes of denial. In fact, the perpetrators had deliberately conflated a political threat from the left with ethnic identity. They had fused a deeply ingrained fear and mistrust of indigenous peoples with anti-communism, generating a paranoid and Manichean view of the world.[31] In their minds, anyone opposing their image of the nation was disloyal and had to be destroyed. The findings of the CEH challenged the fantasy at the heart of their nationalist project and revealed its inherently genocidal consequences. Although to date, no one has actually been punished in either Guatemala or the United States for their orchestration of this crime, the wall of silence that surrounded this genocide has been broken. In Guatemala, at least, it is no longer easy to deny that genocide took place.

# 6    Genocide after the Cold War

## Iraq and the Kurds

### Antecedents and context

Little was done until the end of the Cold War to place the question of genocide back at the centre of international concern. The situation began to change only with the first Iraq War in 1991, when the plight of the Kurds suddenly attracted serious attention. The Kurds, the fourth largest ethnic group in the Middle East, had experienced serious human rights violations at the hands of several other states for decades – the Soviet Union, Syria, Iran and Turkey. There had already been at least one case of genocide, in 1937–8, when between 50,000 and 150,000 Kurds in Dersim (about 10 per cent of the population) were murdered in Turkey.[1]

There was a long history of conflict between the Kurds and a succession of regimes in Iraq, but it was not until the advent of Saddam Hussein's Baathist one-party state that it turned to genocide. This state had several totalitarian features: a single party; a supreme leader; a monolithic ideology; and an extensive terror apparatus, spreading quite intense fear and dread throughout the society.[2]

Rebellions by the Kurds in the past had generally concluded with negotiations and some kind of peace accord before the fighting began again. What changed in Iraq was a radical and brutal new policy of Arabisation pursued by Saddam from the 1970s onwards. Up to a quarter of a million Kurds were displaced as the regime sought complete control of oil in the Kirkuk region. Many fled into Iran, which was attacked by Saddam in 1980, starting the brutal Iran–Iraq War that lasted eight years. The Kurds (naturally enough perhaps in the circumstances) allied themselves with the Iranians. This enabled Saddam to claim that he was simply pursuing a counter-insurgency strategy against a 'fifth column'. In 1983, Saddam launched a mini-genocide in 1983 against the Barzani clan, whose head was one of the Kurds' historic leaders. All males between the ages of 7 and 70 were targeted and some 8,000 murdered from this one extended family.

## Victims

### An eyewitness account of the *Anfal*

They brought us to a big and long hall that had space for all the residents of a village ... there was a series of the halls ... military trucks and minis and big buses brought other people continually.

I cannot describe this situation and this sight to make you see how they brought other peoples and treated them as animals ... you could see a solder beating people with his gun, you could see a woman kissing a soldier's shoes because her child was taken by him as he kicked the woman back ...

In the first night, they came and took the young men from our hall, throwing them outside, I don't know to where? ... women's screams and children's cries could deafen heaven ... the second night they came and took all the children ... like wolves which attack sheep, in this way they attacked us ... the next morning they brought the children back ... but children were terrified and freezing, they could hardly breathe.

The third night they separated the elders from us, they put us in the covered buses ... here many mothers and daughters, fathers and sons, women and men were separated ...

We were around 300 women plus the children in each hall ... we had very little space, like we were sitting on each other like sheep and goats ... think! in a few days they burn your house, separate your husband, take young girls, throwing you in a hall like dead bodies ... people say that cats have seven lives, but this is not true, we have seven lives since we did not die ...

When the government released us and we came back, people told us that we were Anfalized; we did not hear the word until that time.

(From an interview conducted by Arif Qurbani (2004) in Kurdocide Watch – formerly Center of Halabja against Anfalization and Genocide of the Kurds (CHAK), *'Anfal', The Iraqi State's Genocide against the Kurds,* 2nd edition, http://www.kncsite.com/Anfal.pdf, accessed 19 April 2004.)

What happened to the Kurds marked perhaps a new low in the history of genocide since 1945, bringing back echoes of the Holocaust. For the first time a state used chemical weapons against its own people.[3] The first attack was on the town of Halabja on 15 March 1988, when the Iraqi air force dropped mustard gas, nerve and blood agents on an unsuspecting population. These caused immediate death, skin and eye burns as well as long-term medical problems, including cancers, birth defects and infertility. Five thousand people were killed and more than 10,000 injured. The effects have been compared to those experienced by people living one or two kilometres above ground at Hiroshima and Nagasaki.[4]

This attack was technically separate from the full-blown genocide of the so-called *Anfal* campaign which lasted from February to September 1988, in which between 50,000 and 100,000 civilians were killed. Four thousand villages were destroyed (out of a total of fewer than 5,000), through shelling and bombing, with repeated use of chemical weapons. The villages were surrounded by troops who then looted, destroying mosques, schools and power supplies, poisoning wells and burning crops, before sowing landmines to ensure no one could return. Fleeing villagers were captured *en masse*. Many were executed immediately by firing squads, either in pits or thrown into them after being shot. They were then buried in mass graves dug by bulldozers. Survivors were transported to concentration camps where they were segregated, interrogated, tortured. Many starved there in overcrowded and insanitary conditions. One and a half million were deported far away from their homes to 'model villages'; 60,000 more fled the country. Even after an amnesty was proclaimed by Saddam at the end of the *Anfal*, many more Kurds disappeared.

## *Perpetrators*

The man who gave the orders for the genocide was Ali Hasan al-Majid, known as 'Chemical Ali'. He was a cousin of Saddam, who had given him extraordinary powers as secretary of the Baath's Northern Bureau to deal with the Kurds. Other leading perpetrators were top generals of the army and directors of security forces. The main organisations which carried out their orders included: the 1st and 5th Corps of the army; commando units; the air force; the Republican Guard; the *Amn* (State Internal Security); the *Istikhabarat* (military intelligence) and the *Mukhabarat* (Baath Party intelligence); and Baath Party militia forces. All reported regularly both to al-Majid and Saddam.

The *Anfal* was a tightly run centralised campaign, involving eight sequential sets of attacks in six distinct geographical areas. It lasted from February to September 1988. Although Saddam's regime has sometimes been presented as a secular one, it was not averse to invoking religious elements. The name *Anfal* comes from the eighth chapter or *Sura* of the Koran, where it refers to spoils or booty of war, and the plunder of the infidel.

The ideology of the regime, however, was not fundamentally religious but rather a compound of nationalist, racist and Stalinist elements. Even before the bloody coup which brought him to supreme power, Saddam had said that 'when we take over the government, I'll turn this country into a Stalinist state'.[5] The *Anfal* was intended as a 'final solution' to the Kurdish problem and the mass executions have been likened to the activities of the Nazi *Einsatzkommandos* in Eastern Europe.[6] Kurds were routinely described as 'donkeys' or 'dogs' or 'human cargo'.

However, this did not prevent the regime coercing some Kurds into acting as collaborators, formed into the *jahsh* (national defence battalions), though they were never fully trusted by the regime and were poorly equipped. In some cases, they may have helped their fellow Kurds to escape.

### Intent

The *Anfal* clearly destroyed a substantial part of the Kurdish people in that area. In a meeting in May 1991, al-Majid himself rejected claims that 180,000 had been killed but only by boasting that the total number could not have been more than 100,000![7] An immense set of documents was captured by Kurds after the first Gulf War in 1992; many more were found after the toppling of Saddam in 2003. The Baathist regime was quite compulsive in keeping records of what it was doing.[8] A document numbered 28/3650 on 3 June 1987, issued by al-Majid, gives the instruction to 'kill any human being or animal present' in any area prohibited to Kurds; another, dated 23 June 1987, to 'carry out random bombardments ... at all times of the day and night in order to kill the largest number of persons': 'those between the ages of 15 and 70 must be executed'. Another, dated 1 April 1987, talks of 'the total elimination of villages'.[9]

As the extensive Human Rights Watch investigation showed, 'many features of *Anfal* far transcend counter-insurgency':[10] large numbers of Kurds were killed; serious bodily and mental harm was caused; and the assault on the infrastructure of Kurdish life was deliberately calculated to bring about physical destruction.

## Rescue, intervention, aftermath

The genocide came to an end again in this case when the perpetrators had had enough. Saddam even held a 'victory' celebration in Baghdad. Few in the outside world had shown any interest. The United States was far more concerned at the time with Iran and saw Saddam as a key ally in the region; neither the Soviet Union nor China protested nor did any state in the region, where Arab or Turkish or Iranian nationalists saw the Kurds only as a problem. There was a very limited protest about the use of chemical weapons by George Schultz, the Secretary of State, but only when the *Anfal* had ended, and long after the US government had extensive knowledge of what the Iraqi state had been doing.

What changed perceptions was Saddam's invasion of Kuwait in 1990. Violence against another state was clearly a different matter. Inside Iraq, the remaining Kurds were again seen as a potential fifth column, and many more were killed. This time, however, publicity was given to Kurds now trying to flee Iraq and, belatedly, a no-fly zone was introduced by the Americans and British over the region. The same protection was not given to another target of the regime, the Marsh Arabs of the south, against whom another genocidal attack was launched, with bombing and then the draining of the marshes. This was both an environmental and human catastrophe, destroying the infrastructure of life for the group.[11]

The Kurds and the Marsh Arabs were finally liberated from the threat of genocide by the toppling of Saddam in the second Iraq War. However, the war was not fought for this purpose and Iraq subsequently disintegrated into civil war, with immense loss of life on many sides, including among the Marsh Arabs. The American occupation was bitterly attacked by many as an instance of imperialist violence, and the problem of genocide was largely forgotten, though not by the Kurds. Even in the mayhem of post-Saddam Iraq, efforts were made to bring some of the perpetrators to trial for genocide. Saddam was not convicted however for the crime of genocide of the Kurds but rather for executing 148 Shi'ites from an opposition political party. The *Anfal* charges were dropped against him after his execution. Al-Majid and others were nevertheless convicted for this crime and executed.

The trial was the first time that perpetrators had been tried for genocide inside their own state. However, it has been criticised for not being sufficiently removed from the American occupation, for failing to abide by several basic judicial standards and for the chaotic nature of the proceedings.[12] On the other hand, the international community had done nothing to bring the perpetrators of genocide to justice.

# Yugoslavia 1992–9

## Antecedents and context

The violence that engulfed Yugoslavia in the 1990s was more complex in some ways than the other cases discussed so far. Yugoslavia was a communist state but had broken from the Soviet bloc shortly after Tito led a Partisan movement to victory at the end of the Second World War. The new state was the successor to the first Yugoslavia established after the First World War, which had experienced significant tensions between political leaders of different ethnic groups. When Yugoslavia was invaded by the Nazis, the country was divided and puppet states set up in Croatia and elsewhere. In the civil war that followed, there were terrible atrocities, particularly against Serbs by the Croatian Ustaše fascist regime. Tito was determined not to allow communist Yugoslavia to fall prey to ethnic divisions again. On the one hand, nationalist movements were suppressed; on the other, Yugoslavia was organised as a federal state, composed of different national republics – Serbia, Croatia, Slovenia, Bosnia, Montenegro and Macedonia. However, these republics were not ethnically homogeneous. A significant section of the population of Croatia was Serb; inside Serbia there was the autonomous region of Kosovo, largely composed of Albanians; Bosnia in particular was inhabited by several different groups – especially Muslims, Serbs and Croats.

After Tito died in 1980, the communist state, like others in Eastern Europe, entered a systemic crisis. The republican leaderships were unable to resolve their differences, as elites pursued their own interests and turned to nationalism to mobilise support. In Serbia, one communist apparatchik, Slobodan Milosevic, saw the potential on a visit to Kosovo where he had been sent to dampen down Serbian nationalists. Instead he told them, to rapturous applause, that he deeply sympathised with them and (emboldened by his discovery of this tremendous source of support) returned to Belgrade to take over the ruling Communist Party.

Already inside Serbia, increasingly radical nationalist ideas were being openly promoted. In 1986, a group of Serbian intellectuals had produced an inflammatory 'Memorandum', asserting that Serbs had been oppressed in communist Yugoslavia, even though they were the largest group. In particular they focused on Kosovo, which in Serbian nationalist mythology had a special place as the site of a historic and tragic defeat at the hands of the Ottoman Empire in 1389, and where they claimed the Serbian minority was supposedly now facing 'genocide' at the hands of an Albanian majority.

Milosovic now moved to clamp down brutally on the rights of Albanians in Kosovo and then to try to assert Serbian control of federal Yugoslavia as a whole. This Serbian nationalist project was resisted – first by Slovenia, the one ethnically homogenous republic. After a brief, unsuccessful invasion by the JNA, the (supposedly) Yugoslav National Army, Slovenia was allowed to secede. Milosevic had by now adopted what was effectively Plan B, the creation of a Greater Serbia. Nationalists in Croatia, led by Franjo Tudjman, fearing Milosevic and with their own ambitions, tried to follow the Slovenian example. Serbian nationalists, however, mobilised the large Serbian population in Croatia, invoking memories of what had happened to Serbs at the hand of the Ustaše. A violent war began, with terrible atrocities against civilians, committed largely by Serbs against Croats but to which Croatian nationalists also responded.

## Bosnia

What was to follow, first in Bosnia and then in Kosovo, was far worse – genocide, although this is disputed and depends again on how narrow a definition is adopted. Bosnia was a kind of mini-Yugoslavia itself, a multi-ethnic society, which in itself was anathema to Serbian nationalists. They had a particular animus against the capital Sarajevo, a thriving, multi-cultural city, whose citizens were subjected to a vicious and terrifying siege for three years. Bosnia had to be dismembered. Those who did not want to be part of Greater Serbia (or Greater Croatia) had to be removed, as the society was to be reconstructed according to their radical nationalist vision. The Muslims of Bosnia were a particular target. They were seen as either 'really' Serbs or Croats, who should now return to the religious and nationalist fold, or be forced out. At best, a few might be permitted to congregate in a tiny rump state.

## Victims

### From a survivor's account of the Srebrenica massacre

I was one of the first people brought to Omarska. After ten days, there were 20,000 prisoners …

For the first ten days they didn't give us any food. Then they fed us once a day at 6.00. They gave us three minutes to come from our building to the kitchen. Some of us were more than fifty metres away, and we had no chance to reach the kitchen. Those who came had three minutes to eat. Those who did not had no food. The guards formed a line that we had to get through to get to the kitchen. As we ran they beat us with guns, wheels, and tools …

Sometimes they put us in a 4 x 4 meter room – 700 people. They told us to lie down and they closed the windows and the doors. It was summer. We lay like sardines in a can. Those on top were in the best position. Every morning some on the bottom were dead. Every morning a guard came with a list and called people's names. Those they brought out never came back.

One day they came at 3 a.m. and they brought out 174 people. I was with them. They lined us up behind a building they called the White House. Ten soldiers came with automatic weapons and they started to shoot us. Only three of us survived.

The worst event was when I watched one young man as they castrated him. Right now I can hear his cry and his prayers to be killed. And every night it wakes me. He was a nice young man. His executioner was his friend from school. He cut his body and he licked his blood. He asked him just to kill and to stop all that suffering. All day and night we heard his prayers and his crying until he died. This is something that I cannot forget. It gives me nightmares and makes sleep almost impossible. I can't remember the people who were the executioners. For me all of them in those uniforms were the same. I can't remember who was who.

(From Steven M. Weine, *When History is a Nightmare – Lives and Memories of Ethnic Cleansing in Bosnia-Hercegovina*, Piscatawy, NJ: Rutgers University Press, 1999, pp.34–5).

The assault on Bosnia was initially successful, as Serbs occupied 70 per cent of Bosnia in only nine months. But the violence was to last for another three years as Croatian nationalists followed suit, and as the Bosnians desperately tried to defend themselves with far more limited resources. Approximately 0.25 million people died, and some 1.3 million were displaced out of a total population of 4.4 million. The large majority were Muslims who were subjected to a sustained campaign of violence, intimidation and terror. Nothing like this had been seen in Europe since the Second World War. What was particularly shocking was the discovery in the summer of 1992 of concentration camps inside Bosnia, where Serbs were murdering, torturing, starving and raping Muslim men and women. The worst was probably at Omarska but there were several others. Croatian nationalists also set up similar camps, if on a smaller scale. The Bosnians themselves set up a prison too at Celebici where there were also atrocities.

A major aspect of this violence was its gendered character. The first victims were men of a military age. Once they had been separated, concentrated, tortured and murdered, the way was clear to assault women, with mass rape taking place in several places, not just in the camps but in occupied towns and villages. It is estimated that there were between 20,000 and 50,000 rapes.[13]

## Srebrenica

The worst atrocity occurred at Srebrenica in 1995. Some 50,000 people had been crowded into the town for months, where they were supposedly protected by Dutch troops in what the United Nations had designated a 'safe haven'. It proved to be exactly the opposite. In July 1995, the Bosnian Serb army marched into Srebrenica, and the Dutch troops withdrew. Eight thousand men and boys were then separated from their families, taken away and shot. The rest of the Muslim population was then deported, with 20,000 forced to flee in 30 hours.

Faced with clear evidence of this crime, and further shelling of Sarajevo, NATO bombed Serb positions inside Bosnia. At the same time, the Croatian army launched *Operation Storm* and swept through the Serb-occupied part of Croatia, and many Serbs now fled in turn. The Serbian government finally acceded to demands to end the conflict and a conference was held at Dayton in Ohio. Although it did bring peace, the terms of Dayton to some extent rewarded the architects of genocide. Bosnia was effectively divided, although it remained formally one state, between a *Republica Srpska* and a Federation of Muslims and Croats.

## Kosovo

What was not discussed at Dayton, however, was Kosovo. Unlike Bosnia, Kosovo was not a multi-ethnic society but polarised between a large Albanian majority (90 per cent) and a small Serb minority. Further Serb repression and the obvious failure of a strategy of non-violent protest led to an armed resistance mounted by the Kosovo Liberation Army (the KLA). Milosevic now embarked on an even more violent campaign of repression designed to force the Albanian majority out and 'restore' Kosovo to the Serbs. Faced with his refusal to halt the violent repression of the people of Kosovo, NATO attacked Serbia. This triggered a further escalation of Serb violence, with mass deportations of a kind not seen in Europe since the Nazis. Eight hundred thousand Albanians (out of a total population of about 2,000,000) are estimated to have fled into neighbouring countries, and many more were internally displaced. There was mass killing (between 9,000 and 12,000 murdered), alongside torture and rape.[14]

## Perpetrators

The question of responsibility for the violence has been fiercely contested by nationalists on different sides.[15] But it seems clear that radical nationalists in Serbia were the primary perpetrators: the governing elite around Milosevic, the army, the police and paramilitaries. They also mobilised many civilians. The army worked in concert with police and a range of paramilitary organisations, tied to different political parties in Serbia, some even more radically nationalist than Milosevic. The most infamous of these paramilitaries were the Tigers, led by a notorious criminal, Arkan, and the Cetniks, associated with the radical nationalist Seselj. The paramilitaries carried out tasks the army could not be seen openly to perform, particularly in mutilating, raping and terrorising civilians.[16] The vast majority of the direct perpetrators were young men, motivated by many of the factors identified in Chapter 4 – peer group pressure, alcohol, misplaced fear and aggression. The violence was justified in their minds because 'their' group was supposedly threatened, a view rooted in a widely shared Serbian nationalism which saw Serbs as always victims.

## Neighbours

This nationalism was a powerful enough ideology to turn those who had lived as neighbours in a multi-ethnic society for years, in apparent peace and harmony, into killers, rapists and torturers. How could this happen? One answer is that this was because many people experienced what has been described as a 'cognitive dissonance ... a conflict produced by simultaneously holding two sharply conflicting ideas or acting in a way that strongly contradicts one's strongly held beliefs'.[17] Here, nationalist hate narratives which referred to the past were revived in the context of a systemic crisis. These narratives reorganised people's perceptions of the present, so that they came to see their neighbours as 'really' their enemies, as dangerous people who, because of putative past crimes, had to be eliminated. The failure in the former Yugoslavia to work through the trauma of what had happened in the Second World War was perhaps a critical factor in enabling these hate narratives to work so well.

## Intent

These narratives, of course, had to be produced in the first place and then used to mobilise people for genocide. It is not difficult to show

how and where this was done – by the intellectuals who produced the Memorandum, the politicians who organised the rallies and the institutions in civil society such as the churches who gave these ideas their blessing. But even if there were these hate narratives, was there intent to destroy people in whole or in part? This has been a major issue that, for the first time since 1945, courts have had to decide.

In 1993, the UN Security Council created the International Criminal Tribunal for the former Yugoslavia (ICTFY). It was charged with investigating major crimes in the region, including genocide. One major focus was what happened at Srebrenica, where the Tribunal found that genocide did take place and has convicted three men so far, including one general (Krstic), although his conviction was reduced on appeal to aiding and abetting.

The problem with the judgements, however, is that they appear to indicate that genocide took place only in Srebrenica. From one side, it can be argued that even this judgement is too strong because it rests on too broad a definition of genocide. The intent may not have been the destruction of the group but the elimination of a military threat. It was only men of a military age who were murdered. If the intent was genocide, why did the Serbs not kill the women and children they had at their mercy but 'only' deported them? The numbers killed are only a small proportion of the population (about 0.3 per cent). How can this be understood as destruction of a group in part, let alone whole? In any case, where is the evidence of a sustained policy or project of destruction?

From another angle, however, the judgement and indeed the proceedings so far (given how few Serbian perpetrators have been indicted) seem dismally disappointing and inadequate.[18] If there was genocide at Srebrenica, it was committed by those acting on higher orders, from Milosevic in Belgrade and his associates, from Radovan Karadzic, the leader of the Bosnian Serbs and from General Radko Mladic, the commander of the Bosnian Army. All were finally arrested (although it took an unconscionably long time) and taken to the Hague to stand trial. Milosevic unfortunately died before his trial could be completed, but the other two can now be prosecuted. The killing at Srebrenica surely formed part of a wider project of destruction. This was the argument put forward by the Bosnian government but the International Court of Justice (ICJ) decided that Serbia was not guilty of genocide, though guilty of failing to prevent it. But this seems to make little sense if those who are criticised for failing to prevent genocide are the very ones who ordered it.

Part of the problem here may lie in the recurring tension between history and law. Most historians of the Yugoslav wars would argue that there was a policy pursued by radical nationalists which led to genocide. Genocide in Srebrenica and elsewhere in Bosnia and Kosovo was not an accident or coincidence. It was a central part of a nationalist project, which required the destruction of the Muslims of Bosnia and the Albanians of Kosovo.

## Rescue, intervention, aftermath

Political leaders outside Yugoslavia refused to grasp this basic issue for a long time. Many chose to think about the violence as a manifestation of 'ancient hatreds' supposedly deeply rooted in the Balkans, an area it was best to stay well away from. At best, they should try to negotiate some kind of compromise between the warring parties and not further inflame the conflict by giving arms to any side. This had the effect, of course, of leaving the Bosnian Muslims and Kosovo Albanians at the mercy of the well-equipped and Serbian-controlled JNA.

In an attempt to give some protection to civilians inside Bosnia, the UN decided to create a number of so-called 'safe havens', patrolled by UN forces. However, these forces had orders not to engage in fighting and, as Srebrenica showed, would not and could not protect those they were supposed to be shielding. In the end, only the NATO bombing campaign against Serb positions inside Bosnia made a decisive difference, as it did later in Kosovo.

Not everyone, it has to be said, shares this view, especially about Kosovo. Critics (largely on the anti-imperialist left), deeply sceptical of the motives of Western states, have argued first that NATO's intervention in Kosovo was illegal, which it was: the UN Security Council did not agree it, as both China and Russia opposed it. Second, it is said to have produced the very genocide it was supposed to prevent, and it is true that Serb violence escalated when the bombing started (although it was already mounting). Third, the bombing itself caused the loss of innocent life in Serbia, which it did, as NATO attacked from 50,000 feet and refused to send in ground troops (although presumably they would have killed innocent people too). Finally, the outcome in Kosovo was that the Albanian majority, now enabled to return to their homes, showed no desire to live in peace and harmony with their Serb neighbours. Now it was Serbs who experienced repression and revenge attacks from the former KLA, who dominated the political scene. It is estimated that over 150,000 Serbs (and Roma too) fled.[19] Even less than in Bosnia, communities are not living harmoniously in a secure, democratic state or a stable, multi-ethnic society.

However, genocide did not come to an end in Yugoslavia when the killers had had enough but when they were forced to stop. In Kosovo especially, those subjected to genocidal assaults could not protect themselves. Only intervention from outside saved their lives and what was left of their societies and communities. This is not to justify the form or timing of the intervention, or to ignore difficult issues to do with motive and consequence, to which we turn in the next chapter.

## Rwanda 1994

Before we do so, however, we need to look at another case, which took place at the same time – the genocide in Rwanda. Here, almost 50 years after the end of the Holocaust, there was no serious intervention until it was far too late. The result was a catastrophe that still beggars belief – the murder of around 800,000 people in three months, a rate of killing three times as fast as the Holocaust.

### *Antecedents and context*

Here genocide was again committed by a post-colonial state. Pre-colonial Rwanda was a quite stratified, hierarchical society, with a population composed of two main groups – Hutu and Tutsi. These categories were fluid, based largely on wealth and power. Hutu and Tutsi were not different 'tribes' but spoke the same language, shared the same culture, intermarried and lived in mixed communities. People could move in and out of these groups quite easily.

What radically altered the meaning of these categories was European occupation and exploitation. The first colonialists were the Germans, who introduced racist theories in an attempt to link differences in wealth and power to purported physical differences, such as height or brain size or length of nose. The Germans were succeeded after the First World War by the Belgians, who used the racialised distinction to divide and rule through a Tutsi elite and to control the population through a system of identity cards. An important role in spreading racist theory was played by Church missionaries, who proposed that the Tutsis were descended from the biblical figure Ham, and had come down to Rwanda from the Nile. However, as the decolonisation process began to sweep away European direct rule, the Belgians switched sides, suddenly promoting Hutu interests.

In 1959, there was a violent revolution which swept the Tutsi elite from power. Between 20,000 and 100,000 Tutsis were killed. Rwanda became independent in 1962 and there were further assaults, as Hutu nationalists sought to reverse the political, social and economic dominance of the Tutsi minority. This presents a particular problem for the study of genocide. In this case, mass killing was the outcome of a revolution which created a new independent nation state and overthrew the rule of a minority, previously complicit with the colonial power. How could the pursuit of such a progressive cause result in the worst genocide since the Holocaust?

There are several potential answers to this question but it is clearly nonsense to see it as the result of deeply rooted tribal divisions or long-standing ethnic hatreds. There were no 'tribes' and the ethnic differences were exaggerated, reified and racialised only quite recently. Without identity cards, it would have been much harder to say who was Hutu and who was Tutsi. Some have argued therefore that the genocide is best understood within an anti-imperialist frame of reference;[20] or as a case of 'subaltern genocide', whilst Michael Mann sees it as an example of the 'dark side of democracy'.[21] It needs to be remembered, however, that these differences were enthusiastically adopted by the *génocidaires*. It was their decision to use them to identify the group to be killed which was critical.

An important dimension, however, is also regional. Neighbouring Burundi exhibited many of the same features as Rwanda, with a genocide taking place there in 1972, only the other way round, with about 100,000 Hutus murdered by the Tutsi-dominated regime and, for René Lemarchand, it is this reverse genocide which was decisive.[22] What happened in the region is clearly very important before, during and after the genocide. Many Tutsis were forced to flee Rwanda after massacres in 1959, 1963 and 1973. By 1990, there were around 900,000 Tutsi refugees in neighbouring states. In Uganda, some had gathered together in 1987 to form a rebel army (which included some Hutu), the Rwandan Patriotic Front (RPF) which invaded Rwanda in 1990. Rwanda was now plunged into a civil war, which lends some force to the argument that war and revolution are key factors in the genocide.[23] There was also a serious economic situation, as coffee prices had plunged on the world market which, together with war and revolution, would certainly have constituted the kind of 'difficult life conditions' which Staub emphasises.

Outside powers, especially France, now the key neo-imperialist power, sought to broker a resolution of the conflict. President Habyarimana was prevailed upon to sign a peace agreement at Arusha in Tanzania in August 1993. This, however, did not include key radical elements on the Hutu side (advocates of Hutu Power), nor was it adequately backed up by what was only a limited UN presence.

A few months after Arusha, President Habyarimana's plane was shot down, in murky circumstances which are still debated. In any event, the assassination of the president, which carried echoes of the assassination of the president of Burundi in 1993, was the catalyst for genocide. Hutu Power nationalists filled the vacuum and began to implement their plan to eliminate the Tutsis once and for all.

*Victims*

### A survivor's account of the Rwandan genocide

On Thursday afternoon, soldiers arrived. After that it was calamity. As soon as the soldiers arrived, they started shooting. Everywhere, there was a hail of bullets, bullets, bullets. People started dropping dead. The cows fled ... Then the interahamwe came and started macheting and spearing ... Some of us tried to run away while all around us people were dying and falling down. I left my children and husband behind. All you could think of was surviving. In fact you did not think. You just went with your fear and your legs. As you ran, you had to step over the bodies that were falling all over the place. Hundreds and hundreds of bodies lay scattered everywhere, lying in every twisted position you could imagine. All around, there were cries for help, and sometimes only whispers because people were so hurt. But there was no question of stopping ... We hid in a small bush. We were in a group of about fifty. We hid until about 11.00 p.m ... We walked the whole night. I cannot claim I knew where I was going. I just moved with the others. We passed several roadblocks, fortunately at that time of night, they were not occupied. We had just about reached the Kanyaro River, at about 4.30 a.m., when the killers started waking up for their daily work, that is killing ... A mob of about thirty thugs came after us. When they reached us, they started boasting about the number of people they had just drowned in the river ... They started with the men. They took away their money, undressed them and tied them up with their hands behind their backs. They stripped the women down to their petticoats, forcing the babies to cling to their mothers. We were taken to the papyrus swamps. When we approached the swamps, the women were also tied up. They took the two babies off the backs of their mothers and macheted them to death in front of us. Then they macheted the other children to death ... We were marched towards the river. I was the first in line. They beat us in order to force us to jump into the river. I did not want to be macheted. Anything but that. I cannot swim but I threw myself into the river to die by drowning. Two other women also jumped in. The killers macheted two children and then threw them in after us ... I came back to Rwanda on 26 May. I have had no news of my husband and five children or any other members of my family.

(From African Rights, *Rwanda: Death, Despair, Defiance*, revised edition, 1995, pp.356–7.)

The large majority of the 800,000 victims were Tutsi, 75 per cent of the total Tutsi population. There were also a number of Hutu victims, perhaps as many as 50,000, targeted particularly at the outset as moderates and suspected of disloyalty. The genocide was thus also against political groups. The killing was of young and old; men, women, children and babies. Many were murdered by machetes, implements also used for farming in a largely agricultural economy. Many victims were congregated for killing, in schools and even in churches. The killing often took the form of hunting, as the killers searched for victims they knew well, and could recognise personally, since they lived alongside them. Few could escape in such circumstances. In some cases, Hutus killed their Tutsi wives or relatives, even their children.

There was also a very high level of sexual violence. Many women were raped, with some estimates as high as 250,000. More women than men survived but many were infected with AIDS (as are their children) and now live in a 'land of widows'. The Hutu Power ideologues seem to have had an obsession with gender, their particular fury against Tutsi women rooted in the racist discourse they inverted from European imperialists.[24]

The victims were completely dehumanised, not only seen as alien but described as *inyenzi* or 'cockroaches' who had to be cleared from the land. This ideology was propounded systematically, in print and on the radio, in word and in image, accompanying and fostering the escalation of physical violence.

## Perpetrators

The elite who sought genocide were composed of a number of elements. A core group was organised around the president's wife Agathe and what was known as the 'little house' or *akazu*. It was composed of northerners and included her three brothers, the head of military intelligence, the commander of the Presidential Guard and (the leading figure) Théoneste Bagosora, *chef de cabinet* in the military of defence. This group had their own secret organisation, the Zero Network, but could also rely on the close co-operation of the army and state officials at central and local level, where a system of prefects and *bourgmestres* helped organise the killing in towns and villages. The army was central to the initial killings but the greater the distance from Kigali, the greater the part played by local officials and two paramilitary organisations: the *Interahamwe* ('those who work together') and the smaller *Impuzamugambi* ('those who have only one aim'). The paramilitaries were composed of young men, often unemployed or landless, but also reservists and students, and the officers included many professionals (including doctors and teachers). They expanded rapidly, from about 4,000 to 30,000 or even more, as the killing went on. Many appear to have had a considerable enthusiasm for what they were doing. In a series of disturbing interviews, Jean Haltzfeld was told by one group that 'we seized the opportunity. We knew full well what had to be done and we set out to do it without flinching, because it seemed the perfect opportunity'.[25]

What was even more striking than in Yugoslavia was the level of popular participation in the genocide. It has been estimated that 200,000 took part in the killing. This means a large number of ordinary men – and women. They came from all parts of society, young and old, educated, even church ministers. About 97 per cent had Tutsi neighbours; two thirds had Tutsi relatives. They lived alongside them, played football with them, shared food with them in hard times, looked after each other's children, even married and had children with them. Many had no prior involvement in violence. They seem to have been quite average in terms of age, paternity, occupation and even political affiliation.

What turned them into killers? Scott Straus argues that it was not primarily ideology. He lays more stress on situational factors – war and fear of the RPF and of Tutsis returning to power, peer group pressure, fear of punishment and opportunity (to loot or steal property). He identifies what he calls a 'cascade of tipping points'. Once the violence started, a momentum built up which, beyond a certain point, was unstoppable.[26]

Many women too were involved – in killing to some extent but also in denouncing victims, in singing in praise of the killing, in distributing petrol to burn victims to death. Many were professionals too – teachers, councillors, journalists, nurses. Pauline Nyiramasuhuko, who was the Minister for Family, was eventually convicted for genocide and two of the key organisers in Kigali were women.

## Intent

One possible implication of the 'cumulative radicalisation' approach is that the genocide was not necessarily fully planned. The major difficulty with this, as Linda Melvern has conclusively demonstrated, is that there is substantial evidence of planning.[27] There were secret organisations, such as the Zero Network, whose existence had been revealed in 1992. Huge quantities of machetes had been ordered (from China) between 1992 and 1994: they were not required for farming. Paramilitaries had been organised and had been supplied with weapons. Lists of Tutsis and suspect Hutus had been drawn up for when the genocide was to commence.

The killing, moreover, was co-ordinated, not least by radio. *Radio-Télévision Libre des Mille Collines* had been hammering out hate-filled propaganda right up to the time the genocide began, calling Tutsis 'cockroaches' which had to be destroyed. Once the killing started, the station liaised closely with the army command to broadcast specific instructions to people about where to go and who to kill. Alongside this there were hate propaganda magazines, such as *Kangura* which had already in 1990 published the infamous Hutu 'Ten Commandments'. These laid out clear instructions to every Hutu – to see every Tutsi as a traitor, not to trust them, not to do business with them, not to allow them to be teachers of their children, or to serve in the army or the state, and above all not to show them any mercy. It is hard to think that this ideology, consciously adopted and propagated by Hutu Power nationalists, did not have a considerable effect, at least on the enthusiastic perpetrators.

## Rescue, intervention, aftermath

There is one particularly telling piece of evidence about the plan to commit genocide. It was revealed to the commander of the UN forces in Rwanda (UNAMIR), the Canadian General Roméo Dallaire, by an informant in the *Interahamwe*. On 19 January 1994, he told Dallaire that there were plans for the militias to kill civilians in huge numbers, that there were secret weapons dumps, and that there were plans to kill Belgian troops and so force the UN to pull out. Dallaire sent a fax to the UN in New York asking for permission to seize the weapons. This request was rejected, on the grounds that it went beyond the mandate for UNAMIR. The information was not shared by the Secretary General with the Security Council. In a show of force, the *génocidiares* organised the killing of Belgian troops. Belgium promptly sought a total withdrawal of UN forces. The UN then scaled down its already limited force in Rwanda, doing exactly the opposite of what Dallaire asked, which was to give him 5,000 men. Instead, the order was given to evacuate foreigners. Troops were dispatched into Rwanda to do so, ignoring the desperate pleas for help from Tutsis. Events now moved very fast. The prime minister was assassinated and the killing began in earnest. Dallaire and his few troops sought desperately to rescue the few they could, most dramatically in the Hotel Mille Collines, where over 1,000 Tutsi men, women and children congregated. But they could do little to stop the killing.

Meanwhile, at the UN, the United States and Britain did all they could to avoid using the word 'genocide'.[28] A spokesperson for the State Department told reporters that there was a crucial difference between acts of genocide and genocide, although she could not explain what it was. It is clear that the US administration feared that using the term would obligate it to act. It was not prepared to do so, having recently suffered a humiliating experience in Somalia where a few American troops had been killed and the United States had pulled out.

But the United States and Britain were not the only culpable powers. France, after all, had been more deeply involved in Rwanda than any other state. It had backed the regime against the RPF; it had armed the Hutu state and trained its soldiers and probably its paramilitaries; it had extensive knowledge of what was going on. France was paranoid about losing a client state in Francophone Africa.[29] At best, it sought to portray the conflict as a civil war. Finally, faced with mounting pressure to do something, the French suddenly organised an intervention, when the genocide was nearly complete. Operation Turquoise did little, however, to save the remaining Tutsis. In fact it probably did rather more to save the *génocidiares*, who had been routed by the RPF and now fled into neighbouring Zaire, along with large numbers of Hutus who still followed their lead.

In this case the genocide was stopped from without, but by an invasion from exiled members of the targeted group, not by the international community, which had abandoned the victims to their fate. This failure contrasted starkly even with the easily violated safe havens of Bosnia. It was to lead to a major rethink about intervention, which we discuss in the next chapter.

## Justice and reconciliation after genocide

The ending of the genocide in this way, through a successful invasion by the RPF, had major implications for justice and reconciliation. The new government was increasingly dominated by Tutsis, who formed the overwhelming majority of victims but were also the minority who had ruled Rwanda before the revolution of 1959, and ruled too as a minority in neighbouring Burundi. There are no obvious parallels to this situation in the history of genocide since 1945. The KLA in Kosovo were the majority; Jews did not come back to rule Germany and had never had any kind of power before anyway. What kind of justice would the victims seek?

As in Yugoslavia, the UN created a tribunal to prosecute the perpetrators – the International Criminal Tribunal for Rwanda (ICTR). This was set up, however, not in Rwanda but in neighbouring Tanzania. It has been criticised for several failings: for not indicting enough people; for taking far too long; for being very expensive; and for poor organisation. (Some former *génocidiares* found employment in the ICTR itself!) Its defenders have pointed to the fact that a number of perpetrators have nevertheless been convicted, including not only civilians but the former prime minister, Kambanda; that it has now determined that rape is a genocidal act; and that it has prosecuted people for the first time for incitement.[30]

Alongside the ICTR, the Rwandan government set up its own national court to try second-rung perpetrators. However, the prisons were soon overflowing, with 100,000 in jail by 2000. In an improvised solution, the government set up a new system, *gacaca* or 'justice on the grass', drawing on local traditions. This brought perpetrators and survivors face to face in the local community, without lawyers. It is not an adversarial system like the ICTR, aiming for retribution or deterrence, but has a restorative and reconciliatory purpose.

Critics of *gacaca* have argued that the process is deeply flawed; that it has been imposed from above (attendance is now mandatory); that it does not help to promote reconciliation but tars all Hutus with the perpetrator brush. Its defenders point out that it has achieved rather more than any courts in Germany or Austria or Italy after the Holocaust, that it has empowered women in particular and that it has enabled some of the truth to come out.[31]

The truth, however, may not heal such deep wounds, at least not to begin with. This raises the question of whether a degree of amnesia might not be required, just to enable people to rebuild something of their lives on a day-to-day basis. The question of memory runs though into the issue of identity itself, which played such a critical role in the genocidal process from the very beginning. The Rwandan government policy now is to deny the relevance of identity and it has banned any assertion of a Hutu or a Tutsi identity. In 2009, it passed a law making what it calls 'divisionism' a serious crime.

The potential for abuse in a system increasingly dominated by Tutsis is obvious. It is not just that ethnic identity may not simply be decreed away. It is more that this gives the government the opportunity to label any critics as divisionist and to accuse them of undermining the fragile post-genocidal peace. Even some of those who brought the genocide to the world's attention, such as the remarkable human rights activist Alison Des Forges (before her untimely death), were bitterly attacked by the Rwandan government. A number of Hutus, who opposed the genocide and sided with the RPF, have also fallen out of favour as the government, in the eyes of its critics, becomes increasingly authoritarian.[32]

This problem may be compounded by the fact that the serious war crimes alleged to have been committed by the RPF itself have not been subject to prosecution in the ICTR. This contrasts with the trials of Bosnians and Kosovo Albanians alongside Serbians at The Hague, although as we have seen, from the opposite end, there are critics of a possible strategy of 'balance' there.

There is no easy way out of any of this. Genocide has devastating consequences, not only for the victims but also for the survivors, particularly when they have to live alongside those who killed their relatives and friends and neighbours, and when denial is still being sedulously promoted by those who have escaped justice and continue to look for ways to regain power. Finding an appropriate balance between prosecution, conviction and reconciliation is a major test of moral and political leadership. It is hardest of all perhaps, when the outside world, from where so much of the criticism comes, failed so utterly to come to the rescue of the victims in Rwanda at the time. Some understanding of this has helped shape recent reflections on the whole question of intervention, to which we now turn.

# 7 Genocide and humanitarian intervention

There was no intervention by the international community to stop genocide for several decades after the Convention. The 1990s did produce a sea change but, despite the end of the Cold War, the Security Council was still unable to authorise effective UN action. The gravest failure was clearly in Rwanda but even the Kosovo intervention was not sanctioned by the UN.

## East Timor

Shortly after the Kosovo intervention, however, another genocide produced a different response. East Timor had been seized by Indonesia in 1975 at the time of the Portuguese revolution. Over the next few years, the Indonesian army and militias tortured and murdered 200,000 men, women and children in a series of operations with telling code names such as 'Encirclement and Destroy' and 'Final Cleansing'. A higher percentage of the population was actually killed than in Cambodia; hundreds of thousands were forced into concentration camps or otherwise displaced. The aim was to forcibly assimilate the population, destroying the East Timorese as a distinct group, in what could be seen as a new version of colonialism. All of this was ignored by the United States and Australia, both of which went so far as to recognise Indonesian sovereignty, although the UN did not.

Only when economic crisis engulfed Indonesia in the late 1990s, bringing down General Suharto, did things change. The new rulers of Indonesia offered a referendum on East Timor in 1999 but when the population voted overwhelmingly in a 98 per cent turnout for independence, the army and militias launched a campaign of bloody revenge, murdering, raping and looting in an orgy of violence. Around 600,000 out of a population of 890,000 were deported or displaced.

This time the UN did act. Australia offered to intervene to stop the genocide, if the Security Council authorised it (which it did), if there was regional support (which there was) and if Indonesia gave its consent (which was granted). This followed diplomatic pressure from both the United States and Australia, and a threat from the World Bank to suspend $1 billion of aid. A major role was, however, also played by Australian public opinion, especially after the vote.[1] The intervention in East Timor was short but effective and is estimated to have saved up to 10,000 lives.[2]

Inside the UN, there remained a deep sense of shame and guilt over Rwanda. The Secretary General, Kofi Annan, who had himself been implicated in the suppression of Dallaire's 'genocide fax', now urged a major rethink. In a series of speeches, he suggested that the major problem lay with the sovereignty of states. In a report to the 2000 Millenium Summit, he posed the question sharply: 'If humanitarian intervention is, indeed, an unacceptable assault on sovereignty, how should we respond to Rwanda, to Srebrenica ... surely no legal principle – not even sovereignty – can ever shield crimes against humanity'. His conclusion was clear. 'Armed intervention must always remain the option of last resort, but in the face of mass murder, it is an option that cannot be relinquished'.[3]

## Humanitarian intervention

Before looking more closely at the question of sovereignty and related issues, we need to pause briefly to consider quite what the term 'intervention' might mean in the context of genocide. It can take several different forms, from the provision of aid to victims, to sanctions against regimes inflicting the distress. It is not synonymous with military intervention, which actually cannot be humanitarian in the strict sense of the word. Any use of military force will involve the loss of life, and at the core of most definitions of humanitarianism is the relief of human beings from distress.[4]

Military intervention, however, is the primary focus of this chapter. This is not because it is the only form of intervention but because it is the only form which can halt genocide once it has started. Although the Convention does not use the term 'intervention', it calls on not only states to prevent and punish the crime (in Article 1) but also 'upon the competent organs of the United Nations to take such action under the Charter of the United Nations as they consider appropriate' to suppress it (in Article VIII). There is much, as we shall see in the last chapter, which might be done to prevent genocide happening in the first place and to punish the perpetrators but these are different, although clearly related questions, since military intervention does not take place in isolation. It is invariably accompanied or preceded and followed by other forms of intervention, including diplomatic and economic ones.

Only military intervention, however, stops genocide from without, although that is not the same thing as how genocides come to an end.[5] There is considerable evidence, nevertheless, that only military intervention does slow or stop slaughter, once genocide has begun.[6] As Alex Bellamy has concluded, 'however appealing, non-military measures ... have not, historically, sufficed'. 'Once genocide has begun, only war on the perpetrators will bring it to a premature end.'[7]

## International Commission on Intervention and State Sovereignty and the Responsibility to Protect

Annan's question was to be addressed systematically by an International Commission on Intervention and State Sovereignty (ICISS), set up in 2000 through the efforts of the Canadian government. Explicitly asserting that 'we want no more Rwandas', the ICISS sought to reframe the problem of intervention in terms of a new definition of *sovereignty as responsibility* and advanced the notion of a *responsibility to protect* – what became known as the acronym R2P. In its report, issued at the end of 2001, the ICISS argued that states had a major responsibility to protect citizens from genocide, mass killing and ethnic cleansing.[8] If they failed to do so, then the international community should step in, although the ICISS insisted that simply reacting to these crimes was not enough; attention had also to be paid to preventing them in the first place and to rebuilding societies afterwards.

Much of the thinking of the ICISS drew on a well-established tradition of political theory concerned with the question of when, if ever, it is right to go to war and how to conduct it – what is known as Just War theory. Just War theory typically proposes that war can only be waged if six conditions are met:

- there is a legitimate authority
- it is a last resort
- there is a just cause
- there is the right intention
- there is a reasonable prospect of success
- the means used are proportional.

The ICISS report similarly laid down a clear threshold – of irreparable harm being done to human beings with large-scale loss of life (with or without genocidal intent). It set out a clear set of precautionary principles (right intent, last resort, proportional means, reasonable prospects) to be adhered to if military intervention was to take place. It laid out a process whereby right authority could be obtained: the Security Council or, failing agreement there, the General Assembly; or, failing that, regional or sub-regional states; or, finally, 'concerned states'.

This original version of R2P was bold and radical but did not command unanimous approval. Critics could point, for example, to the Western and Christian origins of the arguments. In the changed international context after 9/11, where some were arguing about a 'clash of civilisations' between the West and the Islamic world, this was not an insignificant consideration. Many feared that intervention would be more likely to come from Western states and be mounted against non-Western, non-Christian societies.

There were other difficulties. One had to do with the question of who exactly would authorise intervention. The report recommended that the permanent members of the Security Council should agree not to apply their veto in matters where their own vital interests were not involved, a self-denying ordinance not likely to appeal. There was also the question of how to assess intent. What states might give as the reasons for intervening might not be the 'real' reasons. Nevertheless, the report did win considerable praise from a number of quarters – not just from Annan himself or Western states (in fact the United States was quite lukewarm especially about the veto) but also from some states in the global South. A considerable momentum appeared to be building in its favour. It was then, however, nearly derailed by the second Iraq War.

## Iraq (again)

In the context of genocide, there is some irony about this. Iraq, after all, under Saddam Hussein was a serial perpetrator of genocide. However, there had been no outside intervention at the time of the *Anfal* and the Marsh Arabs had been left to their fate. When the United States a decade later invaded Iraq and toppled Saddam, it generated huge and global opposition. There were a few who defended the invasion at least in part on the grounds that Saddam was a genocidal killer, but for the overwhelming majority, none of the arguments associated with Just War or R2P remotely justified it. There was no just cause, since the main reason given, the claim that Iraq possessed weapons of mass destruction (WMD), proved to be quite false. Genocide was hardly highlighted in the case for war and had taken place too long ago in the past to be invoked now. There was no legitimate authority, since it was not supported either by the Security Council or the UN General Assembly. War was not a last resort, since the weapons inspectors were not allowed to finish their job. The means were not proportional but had involved terrible loss of life for the Iraqi people. The outcome seemed to prove conclusively that the war had not had any reasonable prospects of success.

The result was that the United States, to which some looked to halt genocide, was quite discredited, its legitimacy for any such intervention in tatters.[9] There was now renewed and widespread scepticism about the whole idea of intervention, only ten years after the international community had failed so catastrophically in Yugoslavia and Rwanda.

## Against intervention

The arguments against intervention come from a number of quarters. At one level, they are to do with fundamental questions about international relations. Many scholars in that field are deeply sceptical about intervention. Realists, for example, who believe that states always pursue their own interests and that questions of morality have little purchase in international relations, tend to think that intervention is rarely prudent. Most Marxists believe that supposedly moral arguments for intervention hide altogether baser motives: imperialist states simply wish to continue to control other nations' resources. Pluralists see the international order as a society made up of equal sovereign states, who have agreed to a set of rules to deal with what otherwise would be anarchy. Intervention, in their view, risks undermining sovereignty and the balance of international society itself. Nationalists, in turn, see the nation state as the entity which naturally commands the deepest loyalties and commitments; it is the fundamental guarantor of rights and duties; intervention from outside undermines its necessary authority and power.

Many genocide scholars are also sceptical. Those who see genocide as intimately connected with the history of Western imperialist states are wary of intervention, precisely because of this history. There are more directly political responses too. Much of the opposition comes from states which have in the past suffered the consequences of Western intervention which was the very opposite of humanitarian.

There are then several sources for opposition to intervention. The arguments themselves may be grouped under a number of headings. They have to do with:

- sovereignty
- self-determination

- imperialism
- hypocrisy
- selectivity
- outcomes and consequences.

## Sovereignty

The question of sovereignty is probably the most fundamental. Realists and pluralists argue that sovereignty has provided the essential basis for the international order since the Treaty of Westphalia in 1648, which brought an end to the Thirty Years War in Europe. States then agreed to recognise each other's sovereignty over their own territory. Henceforth, no outside power had the right to intervene in the internal affairs of another state. This agreement is supposed to have stabilised the international order, removing earlier justifications for contesting borders and guaranteeing some degree of peace. International law itself indeed rests in some people's eyes on the very principle of state sovereignty. The UN Charter which established the basis for the post-war international order further consolidated this principle. Article 2(1) proclaims the sovereign equality of all its members. Article 2(7) specifically forbids the UN to intervene in the internal affairs of member states. No state or states is entitled to use force against another, except to defend itself against aggression.

## Self-determination

Politically, the doctrine of sovereignty was given a powerful boost by the anti-colonial movement and the struggle for national self-determination. Non-Europeans had finally won the same rights that many European nations had gained long before. Many of these states joined together to form the Non-Aligned Movement (NAM) and have been amongst the most vociferous critics of any argument for intervention, which they see as a dangerous threat to their hard-won independence. The NAM's immediate response to Annan's speeches in 1999 was that 'the so-called doctrine of humanitarian intervention has no legal basis'.[10]

## Imperialism

It is more though than a question of legality. Self-determination was won in a struggle against imperialism which has had to continue even after formal independence has been gained. Western states continue to press hard on new states, forcing them in all kinds of ways to bend to their will and cater to their interests. The consequences of the policies that they impose on post-colonial states are generally disastrous, driving down living standards, exacerbating internal divisions, fuelling conflicts inside crisis-ridden societies. The very states which, from this perspective, were the original and leading perpetrators of genocide are responsible for the conditions which cause it to occur again. They are surely the last states to be trusted to do something about genocide. If there does have to be intervention, it should only be undertaken by regional powers and not by the West.

## Hypocrisy

When Western states claim to be engaging in humanitarian intervention, they can be accused of several kinds of hypocrisy. One is, as it were, historical. The violence that was often necessary for national liberation, and afterwards to secure sovereignty against internal and external threats, is no different in principle to the violence Western states deployed to construct their own sovereignty.[11] It ill behoves the latter to criticise newly independent states for the same thing. Indeed, if we follow Mark Levene's and Christopher Powell's arguments about the nature and dynamics of the international state system created by Western states (see Chapter 3), the causes of genocide lie in the past and present behaviour *of* such states. Their intervention will do nothing to address the fundamental problems which give rise to genocide in the first place.[12] Their intervention now would hide their fundamental responsibility for genocide, creating or perpetuating a fiction that only other, 'rogue' states commit genocide, when they themselves have been intimately involved in it in various ways throughout their own history (and still are). In any event, when Western states call for intervention now to stop such violence, it is but a smokescreen (handily provided, according to Stephen Werthheim, by neo-conservative ideology)[13] for quite different motives – to extend or reassert the control they had lost when they had been forced to abandon their empires.

## Selectivity

Western states are moreover, it can be argued, markedly selective in the cases they choose for intervention. In the epoch of the Cold War, they did nothing about genocide in the Western sphere of influence (Indonesia, Guatemala). But they also did nothing outside it either (as in the case of Burundi). Now that the Cold War is over, they are not constrained by Soviet opposition but still only seem prepared to intervene when their own interests are at stake. Rwanda had no oil, no raw materials that were at risk. The victims of the Rwandan genocide were too poor, too black, too far away to count. Iraq by contrast had oil, which the West urgently needs. When Saddam was still seen as a useful counterweight to Iran, a blind eye was turned to the genocide of the Kurds. Only when he could no longer be trusted did his victims become a sudden concern.

## Outcomes and consequences

But even when victims of genocide do become a focus for belated attention, military intervention (it is argued) will not produce the outcome its advocates proclaim. The violence it involves brings with it destruction, mayhem and chaos. In Kosovo indeed, it has been claimed that it was the catalyst for the very genocide it was supposed to be preventing. If this was not intended by NATO, it indicates a catastrophic lack of care and preparation, a failure to anticipate what could have been foreseen. Part of this, according to Alan Kuperman, has to do with 'wishful thinking', an unrealistic view of what can be achieved. Kuperman argues that Dallaire's request for more troops in Rwanda would not have saved anything like the number of lives he claimed.[14]

It may also be to do, however, with the manipulation of outside powers by rebel groups. In Kosovo, the KLA provoked the Serbian state to take genocidal action, expecting NATO to be then forced to intervene on their behalf, which is what happened. But the genocidal 'retaliation' would not have happened, Kuperman argues, if this expectation had not been raised in the first place. NATO's intervention helped the KLA come to power (with consequences in turn for the human rights of Serbs in Kosovo), but it did not protect civilians, who paid the heavy price. Kuperman argues that this is an example of a 'moral hazard that encourages the excessively risky or fraudulent behaviour of rebellion by members of groups that are vulnerable to genocidal retaliation'. A norm of intervention 'thereby causes some genocidal violence that otherwise would not occur'.[15]

## For intervention

There are, however, some counter-arguments. Within international relations theory, Solidarists, for example, argue that international society is about more than relations between states; there has to be a concern too with the rights of individuals, groups and indeed humanity as a whole, which may demand intervention in the internal affairs of states. Cosmopolitans take this further, focusing more centrally on the universal rights of all human beings, who may have to be protected from their own states. Constructivists argue that the norms and values which underpin international society evolve over time, and may now legitimate intervention in a way they did not before.

Some approaches to genocide also point towards a more favourable attitude to intervention. Those who lay the stress on particular kinds of states (totalitarian ones, for example) or ideologies, might be more inclined to look to argue that other states (democratic ones, particularly) have a responsibility to act to prevent or halt genocide. Politically, arguments for intervention have come less from states and more from global civil society, from transnational campaigns whose audiences and loyalties transcend the concerns and boundaries of the nation state.

### Sovereignty – and human rights

The pioneer of genocide scholars, Leo Kuper, focused on this from the beginning. In a devastating critique of non-intervention in several cases, from Biafra to Paraguay to Burundi to Cambodia to Uganda, Kuper argued that it was the sovereignty of the territorial state which gave it 'the right to commit genocide, or engage in genocidal massacres, against peoples under its rule, and that the United Nations for all practical purposes, defends this right'.[16]

The concept of sovereignty, it has also been argued, may not provide as secure a basis for states to resist intervention as many might like to think. On closer inspection, sovereignty is not a simple or clear-cut idea but a historically constituted and constantly evolving concept. The Treaty of Westphalia was but one moment in a long-running process. Moreover, what happened at Westphalia is open to different interpretations. One recent historian claims that 'the concept of Westphalia as originating a system of states whose sovereignty was absolute simply is not true'.[17]

If the UN Charter did consolidate sovereignty in some ways, it also constrained it through its repeated references to human rights. This reflects a growing concern, marked at the outset by the UN's own Universal Declaration on Human Rights. Since then the understanding and scope of human rights has steadily expanded, from legal, civil and political to social and economic, and from the individual to the group. The result, as the ICISS argued, is that sovereignty can no longer be seen as absolute but exists to protect human rights themselves.

## Nationalism and self-determination

The right too to self-determination can be seen as problematic, even in the case of post-colonial states. In a number of cases, their borders were bequeathed by imperialism. Within these borders many groups were brought together, not exactly willingly and, as Kuper argued, there were often deep structural inequalities between them which provided some of the conditions for genocide. Whether these different groups could or should form a nation together or were nations themselves, entitled to their own nation state, can itself become the critical issue. Nations are slippery subjects – they are constructs, 'imagined communities' as Benedict Anderson famously described them.[18] They can be imagined in different ways and sometimes in ways that can lead to genocide (see Chapter 3), when radical nationalists states decide that a particular group never belonged to the nation in the first place, and constitutes an internal threat to its very existence. But whose existence exactly? As Michael Walzer has put it, 'when government turns savagely on its own people, we must doubt the very existence of a political community to which the idea of self-determination might apply'.[19]

## Selectivity

There may be a more serious problem than selectivity. It is not, after all as if states are, as Michael Byers and Simon Chesterman have put it, 'champing at the bit to intervene'. The problem seems to have been almost the opposite, an 'absence of the will to act at all'.[20] As we have seen throughout this book, powerful states have generally not seen it in their interest to intervene or even been prepared to acknowledge that genocide is taking place at all.

## Consequences, motives and intentions

Can states come to see intervention as in their own interest, however, and would this necessarily invalidate it? Some have argued that such intervention can still be defended on consequentialist grounds.[21] If the outcome of the intervention is that genocide is halted, this could make it right, even if the motives were not the right ones. From the point of the victims certainly, this seems a very powerful argument. They are unlikely to be that bothered about the motives of interveners, as long as their lives are saved.

There is though a deeper question, which is whether some critics of intervention are not perhaps confusing motives with intentions. James Pattison has argued strongly that there is a vital distinction in this context between the two. 'A humanitarian intervention ... means that the intervener has the *purpose of preventing, reducing, or halting the humanitarian crisis*. Such an intervener acts with the aim of bringing about humanitarian consequences. The *underlying reason* for the intervener's having this humanitarian intention does not, however, also have to be humanitarian. It could be ... a self-interested reason'.[22] This could be a helpful distinction, not least because the demand that states only have humanitarian motives may be rather unrealistic. Most individuals have complex motives for what they do and states are likely to have even more complex motives than individuals.

Moreover, if some motives are self-interested, it could be argued that this might help, since it would mean that states are likely to put more resources into the operation and be more likely to see it through. It may not always be helpful to look to regional powers, who may lack not only the motive (given their anxiety about sovereignty) but also the resources. This is not to say that they should not be given much greater support if they are willing to act. It is rather to be wary of arguments for the deployment of regional forces, if they are used to enable more powerful states to hide behind them and do nothing.

## R2P lite?

These arguments have gone back and forth in recent years, and show little sign of abating. A compromise appeared to be reached in 2005 at the World Summit of the UN which did adopt a version of R2P. In Annan's view, this was a decisive step forward. It meant that the international community was, he claimed, now 'pledged to act if another Rwanda looms'.[23]

Others were not so sure. Thomas Weiss, an adviser to ICISS, has labelled the version adopted at the Summit 'R2P lite', as there are no clear criteria for intervention and states are left to make a decision on a 'case by case basis'.[24] There are two critical differences between the later version and the original one. The first is the withdrawal of the idea that the members of the Security Council should exercise a self-denying ordinance with regard to a veto. The second is that the international community is supposed to intervene, not when 'a state is *unable or unwilling* to halt actual or unapprehended large-scale loss of life or ethnic cleansing within its borders' but when a state is '*manifestly failing* to prevent genocide, war crimes, ethnic cleansing and crimes against humanity'. Perhaps more fundamentally, there is a profound pull back towards the sovereignty principle, evident in the phrasing of paragraph 138. This states that 'each state has the responsibility to protect its populations from genocide ... the international community should ... help states to exercise this responsibility'. Given that it is generally states who commit genocide, this is perhaps rather like saying murderers should be encouraged and helped to protect their victims.

## Darfur

R2P lite or not, the UN soon had a case to test the new doctrine in Darfur, Sudan's largest region, roughly the size of France, where there were mass killings of black Africans by the state (another serial perpetrator). The violence in Darfur is distinct from but connected to the long-running civil war between the government and rebels in the South, which finally ended with a peace agreement in 2003. The issue of Darfur was, however, kept out of these peace negotiations, much as Kosovo was kept out of Dayton. The conflict had erupted in 2003 after decades of mounting discrimination by the government against the main groups in Darfur – the Fur, Zaghawa and Masalit. The rebellion was treated by the government as a 'tribal' problem and met with ferocious violence, which again went far beyond counter-insurgency.

Over the next few years, somewhere between 200,000 and 400,000 were killed – overwhelmingly civilians (95 per cent). Two and a half million were displaced, often to places where there were few means of subsistence. There was systematic destruction of the infrastructure, with whole villages burnt to the ground in a 'scorched earth' policy. Food stocks were destroyed and water supplies contaminated. This was accompanied by extensive sexual violence – rape on a large scale, and the scarring and branding of victims.

The perpetrators of this organised campaign were the Sudanese army and air force working in tandem with militias, the largely Arab *Janjaweed* ('evil men on horseback'). Typically there would be aerial bombing followed by ground assaults by the *Janjaweed,* although the government claimed (wholly unconvincingly) that the militias were not under their control.

The president, Omar Al-Bashir, had been in power since 1989 and had adopted ideology which mixed Arab supremacism and Islamism. This ideology had a distinctly racist dimension, viewing black Africans essentially as slaves in a region where Arab merchants had a long history of buying and selling black slaves. Many of the epithets used to denigrate the victims by the militias evoked this history: 'you are slaves, kill the slaves'; 'you blacks are not human ... you blacks are like monkeys'.[25]

Some have argued, however, that it is a mistake to call what was happening in Darfur genocide. The UN appointed a Commission, chaired by the distinguished Human Rights lawyer Antonio Cassese, which determined that it was not. In its report in 2005, it said it was unable to establish 'beyond reasonable doubt' that there was intent on the part of the government to commit genocide. It argued that the victims were not part of a separate ethnic group, since they spoke the same language as the perpetrators (Arabic) and shared the same religion (Islam). It also pointed to the selectivity of the killing: not all black Africans were being killed when the *Janjaweed* attacked villages. On the other hand, the Commission asserted that calling it genocide should not make a difference. There were crimes against humanity and war crimes, and the international community needed to respond.

However, others have insisted that this is a clear-cut case of genocide. They have argued that there is evidence of intent from the scale of destruction, the pattern of criminal actions, the co-ordination of government forces and militia, racist epithets, sexual violence, displacement in terrible conditions and the killing of large numbers of people as members of a group.[26]

This was also the finding of a US State Department investigation which led, remarkably, the Secretary of State Colin Powell to declare in September 2004 that genocide was taking place. On the face of it, this was real progress, given that it was the reluctance especially of the United States to use the 'g' word that was held to be such a factor in the failure to intervene in Rwanda or Yugoslavia. The problem was that, at the same time, Powell insisted that 'no new action is dictated' by calling it genocide. As Scott Straus puts it, this seems to show that after all 'genocide is not a magic word that triggers intervention'.[27] It is true that the United States did call on the Security Council to act but, given the impasse there, nothing was likely to happen. Neither Russia nor China would authorise action – Russia has sold $150 million worth of equipment to Sudan, including the planes used to bomb villages; China has extensive oil interests in Sudan; both were, again, resolute defenders of the principle of nation-state sovereignty.

They were not alone in refusing to accept the genocide label. Some experts in African conflicts, like Alex de Waal, argue that it is dangerously simplistic and moralistic to use the term genocide. He points out that many African conflicts exhibit similar features or worse in terms of mortality. The killing is part of a counter-insurgency strategy by the state and, in his view, military intervention will not work. The only serious solution is a political one.[28]

Others are even more critical. Anti-imperialists, like Mahmood Mamdani, have argued that the United States was being quite hypocritical, given the carnage it had wrought in Iraq; that Western state powers exhibited no understanding of the complexity of the situation in Darfur for which (as former colonisers) they were in any event fundamentally responsible; and this was yet another case of selectivity, given the equally if not more catastrophic situation in the Congo.[29]

In fact, the United States was not proposing the kind of unilateral action which had aroused so much opposition in Iraq but multi-lateral action from the UN. This was not forthcoming. The UN passed more than 20 resolutions from 2004 onwards but they had little effect. They repeatedly sought the co-operation of the Sudanese government which was itself sitting on the UN Human Rights Commission which authorised the first rather feeble resolution; they placed an arms embargo which, as in Bosnia, only benefited the already well-armed genocidal aggressor.

The UN did, however, authorise a regional force under the African Union. This could have been a real step forward, avoiding the objections to a Western-led force, although there was little appetite for any such intervention from the West, especially the United States, already overextended in Iraq. The problem, however, was that the African Union force was weak, undermanned, underresourced and unable to do much more than monitor the situation. Efforts to bolster it with other non-African troops were rejected by the Sudanese government. Even the peace agreement finally brokered in 2006 only requested the government to disarm the *Janjaweed*.

On the other hand, the UN did refer the situation to the International Criminal Court (see Chapter 8). In April 2007, the prosecutor issued arrest warrants against a *Janjaweed* leader and against the minister for humanitarian affairs (sic). The Sudanese government, perhaps unsurprisingly, refused to give up either man but, undeterred, the ICC then moved dramatically in July 2008 to indict the president himself for genocide as well as for crimes against humanity and war crimes.

Again, serious criticisms have been voiced: that it will be counterproductive, forcing the government into a corner; that it is selective, as the West once again prosecutes only non-Western suspects. The African Union asked the Security Council to suspend the indictments. The NAM has said the indictments will only destabilise the situation further. South Africa, China, Russia and Libya (an important source of support for Al-Bashir) all asked the ICC to set them aside. The Arab League and the Conference of Islamic States also denounced the move.

Throughout this process, the UN has repeatedly referred to R2P as the basis for doing something about Darfur. However, it does not seem to have enabled the international community to act decisively to halt genocide. If R2P alone has not enabled it to do so, what else can be done? It is to this question that we turn in the next chapter.

# 8   Justice and prevention

The prolonged failure to halt genocide was matched for a long time by a similar failure to prosecute and punish perpetrators, even though Article VI in the Convention had called for trials, either in the state where the act was committed or by an international tribunal. There had been the Nuremburg Tribunal immediately after the Holocaust of course, but this was an *ad hoc* military one. In fact the General Assembly did call, on the same day as the Convention, for an International Law Commission to prepare for an international tribunal but its work was suspended once the Cold War started. There were some moves after 1989 to restart the process but the decisive shift occurred with the setting up of the ICTY and the ICTR.

## International tribunals

These Tribunals played a critical role in developing an international justice system able to respond to the crime of genocide, even as the circumstances in which they were set up testified to the failure to halt or prevent genocide in both cases. As Gabrielle Kirk Macdonald (the American judge at the ICTY) put it, 'the Tribunal's creation was simultaneously an act of hope, desperation and cynicism by an international community lacking a coherent policy to respond to the carnage'.[1] It has been argued that they were a relatively inexpensive way to respond to genocide.[2] From another angle, however, they have been criticised for being extremely costly. In 2006–7 alone, the ICTY cost nearly $280 million, a sum which, it has been suggested, could have been used to reconstruct the entire judicial system in the Balkans.[3] Moreover, if the ICTY was meant to deter potential perpetrators, it failed. In some respects the worst cases of genocide were still to come in that region – in Srebrenica and then in Kosovo.

Nevertheless, the Tribunals took the process forward in a number of important respects. To begin with, they reaffirmed the validity and continuing relevance of the concept of genocide itself. Their mandate explicitly referred back to Articles 2 and 3 of the Convention. Second, they were the first international courts to prosecute people for this international crime. The ICTS were set up as subsidiary organs of the Security Council and the judges were elected by the General Assembly of the UN itself. Third, the Tribunals made specific judgements about intent, about targeted groups and about the various acts of genocide listed in the Convention. They also clarified what was involved in command responsibility and the notion of a joint criminal enterprise, judging that it was not necessary for superiors to know in detail what their subordinates were doing but to have a reasonable sense of the risk and likelihood that they would commit acts of genocide. Fourth and perhaps even more fundamentally, in applying the Convention, as Guénail Mettraux has argued, the Tribunals 'liberated genocide from the historical and sociological environment in which it was born ... [and helped establish] genocide as a genuine legal norm of general application rather than as a symbol of a unique historical phenomenon'.[4]

At the same time, the Tribunals moved to close the gap between genocide and crimes against humanity. This did not mean that the significance and gravity of genocide was in any diminished. On the contrary, genocide was specifically and clearly defined in several tribunal judgements as 'the crime of crimes'. Rather it could now be seen as at the end of a continuum, closely connected and related to crimes against humanity. These include murder, extermination, deportation, torture, rape and persecution on political, racial and religious grounds. As William Schabas has pointed out, 'the two categories of crime are cognate ... There have been no convictions for genocide where a conviction for crimes against humanity could not also have been sustained'.[5]

## The International Criminal Court

It seems only logical therefore that the next step should have been the creation of an International Criminal Court (the ICC) even if the process of construction was often fraught politically. After considerable debate, the ICC's statute was agreed in Rome in July 1998 and has now been ratified by as many states as signed the Convention, although not by all the same states. The ICC began work in 2003 and its judges too are elected by an international body, the Assembly of States which has ratified the statute. This lists genocide as the first of the four groups of crimes with which the ICC is empowered to deal; the others are crimes against humanity, war crimes and crimes of aggression. As had the Tribunals, the ICC has adopted the Genocide Convention for the purposes of defining genocide.

A crucial difference with the Tribunals is that the ICC is not an *ad hoc* body set up for a temporary purpose. It is the first permanent judicial body to investigate and prosecute suspects for genocide. Referrals can come from states, the Security Council or the Prosecutor acting on his or her own initiative.

An important source of information, however, for the Prosecutor is the NGO community. This is not an accident. NGOs played a crucial role in pressuring for the ICC in the first place, with a coalition of organisations, including Amnesty, Human Rights Watch, the Women's Initiative for Global Justice and No Peace Without Justice lobbying hard for its creation. In an important sense, this activism testifies to the development of a global civil society (see below). The success of NGOs in forcing the pace of construction of the ICC was perhaps surprising. If the sovereignty of nation states has been as important as has been suggested throughout this book, why did so many states sign up to a court that could potentially prosecute their own leaders?

One answer may lie in the fact that it was states on the Security Council who were most opposed to the creation of the ICC – especially the United States. After Iraq, American unilateralism was a serious concern for many, particularly in the global South. If the new ICC would indeed constrain the United States' ability do what it wanted, perhaps it would have its uses. As it was, opposition from the United States held up the statute for quite some time and even though President Clinton did at the eleventh hour sign up to the ICC, adherence was then revoked by his successor George Bush on the familiar grounds that it threatened American national interests and sovereignty. This was a reprise of the earlier opposition of the United States to the Convention. It is hard, however, to see how this position can be maintained in the long run. It exposes the United States to charges of hypocrisy when it identifies genocide is taking place but then leaves it to others to investigate. This is exactly what happened with Darfur, when the United States was forced to abstain as the issue was referred to the ICC.

Another reason for many states being able to support the ICC may be that a way was found to avert a head-on clash over the question of national sovereignty. The ICC is a court of last resort and is moved to action only when states fail to perform their duty to investigate charges of genocide in their own domain. Even if this is highly likely, it means that the principle of state sovereignty is affirmed in the first place, as indeed it is in the preamble to the statute. The ICC's jurisdiction is fundamentally *complementary* to that of national courts, not a replacement for them.

This important move does not eliminate every problem of course. When nation states do not investigate and prosecute, and especially when they are the obvious suspects, the ICC has to decide what to do. It is at this stage that some of the most acute problems arise. In particular:

- the problem of selectivity
- the problem of peace versus justice
- the problem of what kind of justice
- the problem of punishment
- the problem of process.

## Selectivity

The problem of selectivity has to with which suspects are investigated and why. To date the main suspects have all come from Africa. This has aroused some suspicion. Mahmood Mamdani has claimed that this shows that 'genocide is being instrumentalised by big powers so as to target those newly independent states that they find unruly and want to discipline'.[6] In fact, as even sceptics like Donald Bloxham and Devin Pendas have acknowledged, only suspects in Sudan have been identified by the Security Council, and they have hardly been proactive on the question of Darfur.[7]

## Peace versus justice

The problem posed most acutely by the case of Sudan is a different one. It is whether or not there is a fundamental tension between justice and peace. It can be argued that the decision by the ICC Prosecutor Luis Moreno-Ocampo to indict President Al-Bashir for genocide has set back the prospects for a peaceful resolution to the conflict. Far from ending genocide, it could prolong it. The same argument was made when the ICTY was set up during the genocide and has continued in a different vein since the genocide finished. It can be argued that continuing to pursue perpetrators only makes it more difficult for Serbs and Muslims and Croats to settle down to live harmoniously with each other, as they are constantly being reminded of what happened. The counter argument is that there can be no peace in the long run without justice, that allowing perpetrators to escape punishment fosters impunity.

## What kind of justice?

Answers to this question may depend in part on what kind of justice is being sought in the first place. Benjamin Schiff has suggested that there are two paradigms involved in the debates about justice after genocide, one old and one new. The old one is *retributive*. It focuses on perpetrators as individuals, it is adversarial and it aims to end impunity by making individuals accountable for their actions. The new form is *restorative*. It focuses on the experience of victims, it looks to repair harm and it searches for a broader truth about what happened, enabling a dialogue to take place between the different parties.[8] It is probably the case that the Tribunals and the ICC have leant to the adversarial model, perhaps because of the weight of Western influences. The result has been the application of processes which, in Schiff's view, derive too much from Western traditions of criminal law and which were not designed for the crime of genocide and its impact on the whole of society.

## Punishment

One particular consequence of the influence of such Western traditions is the difficulty with finding appropriate punishment for perpetrators of genocide. This was a problem first identified by Hannah Arendt when she feared that 'for these crimes, no punishment is severe enough ... this guilt, in contrast to all criminal guilt, oversteps and shatters any legal systems. That is the reason why the Nazis in Nuremburg are all so smug'.[9]

The problem here is not just to do with the scale of the killing or the extreme and brutal destructiveness involved in genocide. It is also, as Mark Drumbl has argued, to do with the fact that individuals commit genocidal crimes in a context in which they do not necessarily stand out as deviants. One of the characteristics of the Rwandan genocide, for example, was the level of mass participation. A criminal system designed to isolate individuals and which aims at incarceration may not be able to deal with the problem of a kind of criminality which impacts on the whole of society.[10]

## Process

From another angle, an essentially criminal process may also leave insufficient space for the voices of victims to be heard. This is partly a question of the focus on the accused but also because the process is so largely adversarial. Victims are summoned to appear when they are needed to testify and provide the evidence against those accused. This can be not only risky but also very hard for victims, who may be traumatised all over again as they have to relive the experience.

One way out of some of these dilemmas is to recognise that criminal justice simply cannot deal with all the problems bequeathed by genocide. The damage done is too deep and too great to be resolved by judicial methods alone, at least not those conceived of in criminal or narrowly legal terms. There need to be other mechanisms and processes that can complement the judicial process.

## Truth commissions and transitional justice

Such mechanisms and processes have been developed in some places, in Guatemala, for example, with the CEH. This is one of several similar projects launched in recent years to enable societies to overcome the legacy of mass atrocities and to begin a transition to peace and democracy.

*Truth commissions* perform several functions. Most fundamentally, they provide a record of the past which overturns the perpetrators' version. They paint a bigger picture than criminal courts can hope to do, because they are concerned not just with what particular individuals did but with what happened to society as a whole. Perhaps most importantly, they give centre stage to victims, providing them with a voice which cannot be heard in the same way in criminal trials. Ernesto Verdeja sees truth commissions as 'paradigmatic examples of restorative justice', above all because they give back to victims 'their sense of dignity and self-worth'.[11] Truth commissions restore victims' place in the community as citizens. They now have to be heard and respected as equals, when the perpetrators of genocide had excluded and dehumanised them.

Truth commissions play a central role in what has become known as *transitional justice*. Alongside criminal prosecutions and truth commissions, this involves both reparations and the reform of social and political institutions.

Reparations are important both symbolically and materially; in some ways the former may be more important than the latter. Courts can organise reparations and the ICC itself has now set up a victims' fund. In Latin America, some governments have given payments to families of the disappeared but have also organised memorials and commemorative events. Remembrance is necessary for the victims, so that there can be permanent or repeated public recognition of what happened. It is also necessary for the wider society, so that it can understand how it was itself transformed by genocide.

There is a difficult question though about who reparations should be made to – just to individuals and families or to communities as well? Given that genocide is a crime against groups, it seems logical that reparations should go to the collectivity too. This can take the form of measures which support the reintegration of the group into society, enabling its members to become full citizens, with a range of individual and group rights – not only legal, civil and political but also social and economic ones. This is likely to require significant changes to the way social and political institutions operate, removing or reversing the discrimination and marginalisation which pave the way for genocide. At the very least, there has to be the establishment of the rule of law and of effective controls over the various state apparatuses involved in the genocide. But there are strong arguments that formal, legal and political reforms need to be complemented by social and economic measures which can enable victims to rebuild the fabric of their communities.

## *Reconstruction*

Rebuilding may require the support of the international community. The issue of reconstruction in the aftermath of genocide was, it will be recalled, a crucial aspect of the original R2P doctrine. The commitment to help rebuild was one of the specific criteria proposed for intervention. Although intervention to halt genocide has been so rare, it is clear that war on perpetrators will always involve and add further destruction. This is of course one reason for objecting to it in the first place. If it does take place however, the stronger the argument for rebuilding afterwards. But the converse can also be argued. The greater the failure to intervene to halt genocide, the greater the need to help victims who had been abandoned to their fate. Either way, rebuilding after genocide is an imperative which is gradually becoming acknowledged.

## Reconcilation?

Ultimately, the question has to become one of how groups can live with each other and perhaps the most basic issue question of all – can people from different groups trust each other again after genocide? The damage done by genocide goes very deep and there are many obstacles at several levels to overcome, for both victims and perpetrators. Victims can find it very hard to trust those who come from communities in whose name genocide was committed, especially if actual perpetrators are present or return. This was not generally a problem after the Holocaust, since few Jews survived within or returned to Germany but it is in many societies where genocide has been committed since 1945.

If testifying at truth commissions has a therapeutic function, it is not cathartic, releasing all negative emotions once and for all. Sometimes all that may be possible is to present a mask of mutual acceptance when inside the feelings remain powerful and unresolved. Not every survivor of genocide may feel like the Bosnian women who told researchers that 'we are all pretending to be nice and love each other. But let it be known that I hate them and that they hate me. It will be like that forever, but we are now pretending'.[12] But it would be naive to think that the trauma caused by watching one's neighbours turn into torturers, rapists and murderers does not leave a psychic wound that may never heal.

## Denial

On the other hand, those involved in committing genocide, or who live in communities in whose name genocide was committed, may also find it difficult to admit the wrong that has been done. The more they are confronted, the greater may be the temptation to retrench, to hold fast to the ideologies that justified, legitimated or motivated genocide in the first place. At its worst, the refusal to admit to the crime can be part of a strategy of denial which, as we have seen, is not only the last stage of genocide but often accompanies it from the beginning.

One response to this is to pass a law criminalising denial. There is a precedent for this in laws passed in Germany and then elsewhere specifically in relation to the Holocaust. There has been quite intense debate about this. Defenders of such legislation argue that denial of genocide is not an innocent matter of opinion, but that there is malign intent behind it, which has potentially serious consequences. It is important to protect survivors from further pain but perhaps even more important to prevent denial leading to further outbreaks.

Opponents fear that the cure is worse than the disease. Taking deniers to court gives them more publicity than they should have, paradoxically enabling them to spread their poison wider. There is no easy way to distinguish between differences of opinion or interpretation and what might be seen as denial. The law should not be used to prevent the expression of different points of view about the past. (This is another instance of the recurring tension in thinking about genocide between history and law.) Beyond this, there are serious political issues. It may be too easy perhaps for governments to use accusations of denial to repress opposition, a charge as we have seen that has been made against the Rwandan government in particular.

All of this perhaps shows how deeply damaging genocide is in the short, medium and even the long term. Its effects can be felt not just by those murdered and harmed so irreparably at the time but long after the terrible events themselves. They stretch across generations, poisoning relations between individuals, families and communities over time and place.

## Prevention

The damage wrought by genocide is so immense, the disproportion between the crime and any punishment so great and the difficulties in intervening to halt it so persistent that attention has increasingly turned to how to stop it happening in the first place. Clearly it would be far better, indeed ideal, if genocide could be prevented. But can it?

Given the recurrence of genocide since 1945, after the Holocaust and after the passing of the Genocide Convention, this does seem rather implausible. Many of the explanations discussed in Chapters 3 and 4 have quite pessimistic implications, pointing as they do to deep reasons for why it keeps happening. However, a number of initiatives have come forward in recent years which suggest that, even if it may not be possible to prevent it entirely, much more can be done to minimise the risk of it recurring.

Before looking at some of these initiatives, however, it might be noted that there is a certain paradox built into prevention, which is that the evidence for success is not so much what happened but what did not happen. This is not easy to prove. There is also the problem that the efforts made to prevent genocide are likely to incur costs in the present, when the benefits are going to be felt in the future, and not directly by those bearing most of the costs.

### *Deterrence*

One way of preventing genocide of course is to deter would-be perpetrators. In this respect, the creation of the ICC is an important development. The Rome Statute specifically asserted the need to 'put an end to impunity for the perpetrators … and thus to contribute to the prevention of such crimes'. Before the ICC and the Tribunals, there was a major impunity gap, which is now being filled, although not that many perpetrators have been brought to justice. If the ICC is to perform this deterrent function effectively, it will perhaps have to move rather faster than it has to date, although there has clearly been an important shift in strategy. The ICC began by seeking to prosecute lower-level perpetrators in what was known as a pyramid approach, gradually moving to prosecute leaders of states. The decision to prosecute Al-Bashir indicates that leaders are now being targeted directly, which may have more of a deterrent effect.

### *The United Nations*

The UN too has taken measures which might help. In 2001, the Security Council passed Resolution 1366 which 'acknowledged the lessons to be learned from the failure of preventive efforts that preceded such tragedies as the genocide in Rwanda and resolved to take appropriate action to prevent the recurrence of such tragedies'. It called on the Secretary General to appoint a Special Adviser for the Prevention of Genocide (SAPG), as an Under-Secretary General of the UN. The brief was to:

- collect information on major violations of human rights that could lead to genocide
- act as a mechanism of early warning
- make recommendations to the UN on actions to halt or prevent genocide
- enhance the UN's capacity to prevent genocide.

The first SAPG, Juan Mendez, was appointed in July 2004, following a conference in Stockholm on the tenth anniversary of the Rwandan genocide. Two years later, in May 2006, an advisory committee was set up to assist him.

## Information gathering and early warning

It might be argued that there has not been that much of an information deficit with regard to genocide. There was no lack of information about what was happening in Rwanda, Yugoslavia or Darfur. The problem was and still is an unwillingness to act on the information.[13]

At another level, however, information about past genocides may be useful in identifying when genocide might be likely to occur in the future. Barbara Harff has made a detailed analysis of several genocides and politicides, as she and Ted Gurr call them (see Chapter 2). She has identified 35 such cases between 1955 and 1997 from a total of 126 instances of internal war and regime collapse. She has been able to distinguish with 74 per cent accuracy a set of six 'risk factors'. These are:

- political upheaval
- prior genocide and habituation to mass killing
- exclusionary ideologies and autocratic rule
- ethnic and religious cleavages
- low economic development
- political and economic interdependence (isolated states being more likely to commit genocides).

Harff does not claim that other factors, for which there is currently limited comparative historical data, may not be important, especially the presence of paramilitaries and unrestrained state security agencies. However, she does think that this structural model could enable her to identify which states are currently at risk of genocide. Most of these factors are, as she puts it, 'susceptible to external influence'.[14] If there is monitoring of human rights and help with designing democratic institutions, and if countries could become more interdependent, the risk of genocide could be significantly reduced.

Harff's model is clearly not wholly reliable nor does she claim it would be, but however good the information, the international community still has to decide to do something with it. The international community is made up, of course, of several elements, insofar as it *is* a community at all. In the form of the UN, it is a set of nation states, the large majority jealous of their sovereignty. Inside the UN, power to act lies with the Security Council, which is dominated by Russia, China and the United States, all concerned too with sovereignty, and all with their own history of genocidal violence.

## The United States and genocide – still a 'problem from hell'?

Few people seem to think there is much hope of the former two playing a leading role in preventing genocide but some have looked to the United States to take a lead. This had been Lemkin's hope at the beginning and the failure of his adopted country to ratify the Convention in his lifetime was a bitter blow. Samantha Power made Lemkin the hero of her own history of the United States' repeated failure to deal with the 'problem from hell'.[15] Her powerful and passionate critique has stimulated some important rethinking in the United States, culminating in a major report, produced by a committee chaired by Madeleine Albright (a former Secretary of State) and William S. Cohen (a former Defense Secretary).

The report, 'Preventing Genocide: A Blueprint for US Policy-Makers', came out in 2008.[16] It adopted the term 'atrocity crimes', proposed by David Scheffer (see Chapter 2), and argued that genocide was both a 'direct assault on human life' and a threat to US national interests. Recognising that the credibility of the United States had been damaged, it proposed that it now take a lead in the prevention of genocide. It proposed the creation of an Atrocities Prevention Committee, which could assess risks, using an early-warning approach, to engage with the threat of genocide before it occurred. It should work with international partners in preventive diplomacy, in strengthening norms so that sovereignty could not be used a shield. Military options were not ruled out, not only to halt genocide once it had started but also as a deterrent.

This initiative has met with varied responses. Some have been quite negative, not just because it is not at all clear that genocide is a national priority for the United States, but more profoundly because of America's own record in the history of genocide (including in its own formation). Daniel Feierstein has gone so far as to argue that, given the record of the United States in promoting genocidal practices, the focus should not be on what the United States can do but on what it should '*stop doing*'.[17] On the other hand, Martin Mennecke sees it as 'the first attempt to translate the existing research on genocide prevention into a policy guide for decision makers'.[18] There is a danger that the United States could be damned for what it does not do and then damned for what it does. Even if it is certainly insufficiently self-critical, the 'Blue-print' does represent a significant shift away from previous policy, not to mention the earlier failure to ratify the Genocide Convention. It could also be argued that, in the world as it is currently politically configured, the United States has the most capacity and potential to take a global lead in genocide prevention.

## Regional developments

This is not, of course, to suggest that only the United States can do anything, or that it is always the best placed to do so. There are important initiatives taking place elsewhere at a regional level which may be equally important. One example is the set of regional fora on genocide prevention that have taken place, organised by the govern-ments of Argentina, Switzerland and Tanzania, in 2008 (in Buenos Aires), in 2010 (in Arusha) and in 2011 (in Bern). These brought together scholars, NGOs and diplomats. The aim was to create regionally based networks of states committed to the prevention of genocide. Other initiatives include the setting up of a Regional Com-mittee for the Prevention and Punishment of Genocide, War Crimes and Crimes against Humanity in the Great Lakes, which was established following a pact agreed by several states in 2008.

All of this suggests that prevention is, finally, being taken seriously – by courts, by the UN, by at least one of the great powers and by a number of other states. Perhaps there is beginning to be a significant shift in what we might call the politics of genocide. It is to that we now turn.

# Conclusion: the politics of genocide today

## Scholarship and activism – campaigning against genocide

The involvement of scholars in many of the efforts to develop strategies for preventing genocide testifies to the fact that the study of genocide is not, as Scott Straus has put it, 'a typical field of scholarly enquiry' but one with 'unavoidable normative and ethical dimensions'.[1] This was certainly true for the pioneers, many of whom are still active today. Of course there are difficulties with this. There are bound to be deep, sometimes passionate disagreements about what conclusions to draw from different explanations and analyses, and what courses of action should be taken. But, whatever the differences, there is a general sense that scholarship and activism are and should be intimately connected (see Appendix 2).

Many have turned to the study of genocide in particular after witnessing its consequences and have played a leading role in campaigns to halt and prevent its reoccurrence. Having observed the consequences of genocide in Cambodia, for example, Gregory Stanton (whose work has been mentioned a number of times in this book) set up the Cambodian Genocide Project. Since then, he and other scholars have been involved in a growing number of other organisations, bringing together academics, diplomats, journalists and NGOs.

An important role has been played too by the United States Holocaust Memorial Museum (USHMM), which helped convene the Genocide Prevention Task Force. It provides information about genocide in the world, including eye-witness testimony and a monitor of societies at risk. It also houses the Committee on Conscience, which aims to 'stimulate worldwide action to confront and work to halt acts of genocide or related crimes against humanity'.[2]

## The politics of genocide today

It is no accident that the USHMM has taken on this role. Genocide, after all, came into focus because of the Holocaust, even if it can be argued that it should have done so long before and even if it is a threat which has not been consistently recognised since then.

It is certainly true that several of the genocides discussed here were not acknowledged at the time, and some still have not been. There are others too which never attracted attention in the first place. One obvious reason for this, rehearsed here too at several points, is that the great powers did not wish to give them attention. Cold War strategic priorities and alliances, colonial and imperial interests generally overrode any interest in genocides, when they did not even dictate closer involvement with them.

It is too easy, however, to pin all the blame on the great powers, let alone just one of them. Russia and China have been even more reluctant to recognise genocides in recent years than the United States, but have generally attracted less criticism. Many other states, however, have played their negative part too, as we have also repeatedly seen. This is the case not only for those who have committed genocides (and postcolonial states have been the main direct perpetrators of genocide since 1945) but for many other states in the Non-Aligned Movement, too concerned to maintain the principle of the sovereignty of the nation state and too wedded to the ideology of nationalism.

It may be too easy also, however, to blame only states, who are not after all the only actors in world politics. It was a long time before the question of genocide was taken seriously by civil societies in many of these states. In many ways, this was for some of the same reasons that states typically give for ignoring genocide. In the original nation states of the West, it has been too easy for governments to persuade their citizens that what is happening far away is of no pressing concern. In the global South too, it has not been difficult for states to convince their citizens that responding to genocides is not a priority, when they are preoccupied with trying to secure a stake in that same international order.

There are signs, however, that the hegemonic grip of nationalism, the absolute prioritisation of national over other potential solidarities, is beginning to weaken. The past two decades in particular have seen the emergence of what has been defined as a global civil society,[3] composed of transnational social organisations, movements and networks,[4] mobilising citizens across borders on issues that transcend the borders and boundaries of nation states.

No issue perhaps can be defined more clearly in these terms than genocide. It is within these borders and boundaries that states define and launch attempts to destroy victimised groups of their own citizens. It is only through the invocation of solidarity with fellow human beings across those borders and boundaries that genocide can be halted.

This is not an abstract or purely theoretical argument. There are now several organisations and campaigns which mobilise on a trans-national level to pressure national governments and inter-governmental and trans-national agencies to take action. Some of these played a critical role in the formation of the ICC, whose mandate is to prose-cute perpetrators of genocide, as we have seen. Many have been involved in coming to the aid of the victims of genocide. Some, such as Médecins sans Frontières after Biafra or the Aegis Trust after Kosovo, were even formed in response to particular cases of genocide. Others are involved, as we have also seen, in a variety of international, regional and national initiatives to prevent genocide in the first place.

This global civil society has many constituent elements, but it includes academics, students and informed citizens. Their knowledge and understanding can help generate new ideas, and provide analysis, information and advice to policy-makers, as they struggle with a pro-blem that is not only an immediate threat to a particular set of victims at any one time but also inherently to humanity itself.

### Résumé

This after all was in many ways Lemkin's original starting point, as we saw in Chapter 1. It was his realisation that the modern nation state had the capacity to destroy the inherent diversity of humanity that led him to formulate the concept of genocide. In developing the concept of genocide, he gave the crime a name. In lobbying for the Convention, he worked with others to identify what the crime involved, who was likely to commit it and who had the responsibility to respond to it.

Of course he did not solve every aspect of the problem and the Convention is problematic in certain respects, as we saw in Chapter 2. It is true that it took a long time, an unconscionably long time perhaps, before the international community could stir itself to respond. The Convention, one might say, has been far more honoured in the breach than in the observance. It remains, however, the indispensable point of departure for thinking about the problem and for responding to it. For all its weaknesses, the Convention did make genocide a crime: it spe-cified what the crime entailed ('acts of genocide'); it identified at least some of the groups that could be targeted; it gave some indication of likely perpetrators (states); it laid obligations on the international com-munity to halt or prevent it; and it proposed ways of bringing perpetrators to justice. It is true that there are uncertainties, ambiguities and arguably unreasonable limitations in some of the wording. Subsequent findings by tribunals and the ICC have done much, however, to clarify and resolve these issues, as have complementary judgements on crimes against humanity. Scholars and activists too have helped move the process forward, with various proposals for sharpening the definition of genocide, for broadening its remit to include political and social groups and for connecting genocide more effectively to other 'atrocity crimes'.

Much has been done too to enhance our understanding of the problem of how, where and why genocide takes place. As we saw in Chapter 3, we now have a number of explanations for how it is possible for state elites to come to the decision to eliminate groups and for societies to develop genocidal tendencies and dynamics. We know that there are different kinds of genocide but that certain contexts (war, imperialism, a competitive international order, for example) facilitate its occurrence and recurrence.

We know too much more, as we saw in Chapter 4, about why and how people can become perpetrators but also why others (a much larger number in every case) allow them to do so through their collusion and indifference. At the same time, there is a growing recognition that rescue is possible, not just that there are some courageous individuals and communities who do resist the genocidal tide but that, given a range of political, social and economic circumstances, many others too can act to help victims.

There is nevertheless a limit to what rescuers inside a society where genocide is taking place can do. Once genocide has started, only intervention from without can halt it. This was rarely the case for decades. As we saw in Chapters 5 and 6, genocide has recurred several times since 1948, both during the Cold War and since. It has happened across the world, in Asia, in Latin America, in the Middle East, in Europe, in Latin America and arguably in both Australia and North America too, sometimes continuing dynamics set in motion before 1945 but sometimes setting new ones in motion, and always involving conscious choices and decisions.

The repeated recurrence of genocide did, as we saw in Chapter 7, eventually generate efforts to find ways of intervening to halt it from without. If these have proven very contentious and have stalled to some extent, leaving contemporary victims still at the mercy of perpetrators, there have nevertheless been other developments, particularly in terms of efforts to bring perpetrators to justice and to try to prevent genocide occurring in the first place, which were the primary focus of Chapter 8.

Both the recurrence of genocide and the (belated) emergence of different ways of responding to it mean that the study of genocide cannot stand still. There is now a fast growing literature of different kinds,[5] which continues to throw new light on the subject, both from historians[6] and from several other disciplinary perspectives.[7] At the same time, new case studies are appearing, some on new cases, others bringing attention to more neglected ones, paying increasing attention to the voice of survivors and witnesses.[8]

This is an important development, and again follows developments in the study of the most radical case of all – the Holocaust, the event which triggered the need both for the concept and for the Convention. Where the voice of survivors of genocide may once have been somewhat mistrusted as a source of evidence, there is now a widespread recognition that we need to pay close attention to how it felt to the victims and how it appeared to witnesses at the time.[9]

## In conclusion

For however complex the processes through which genocide develops, and whatever the differences between particular cases of genocide, it has always to be remembered that they are victims and witnesses of a crime, indeed the 'crime of crimes'. It is a crime which, as I have highlighted here, is committed by conscious agents who know what they are doing, certainly since the Convention which identified the crime itself.

For all its faults, the Convention was, I have argued here, a turning point, a critical moment in the making of the contemporary world. It created a new political, legal and moral context in which the attempt to destroy a group was clearly identified and understood as a crime in international law. Those who commit genocide now (above all elites in control of sovereign nation states) know what this crime is, which is one important reason why so often they engage in denial before, during and after they have committed it. Legally and morally, they can no longer hide so easily behind the protective barrier of the sovereignty of the nation state, even if politically they have often sought to do so and too often succeeded. In the contemporary world they can (and now not only in principle, as we saw in Chapters 7 and 8) be held accountable for acts of genocide, which were defined in the Convention and have been clearly understood by tribunals and courts. However hard it can sometimes be to prove, they are acts committed by conscious agents with the intent to destroy other human beings, because the perpetrators see them as members of a group, a group which they wish to eliminate once and for all from 'their' nation, 'their' state and 'their' society.

As I have also argued, the attempt to destroy the group is not only a problem for those particular victims and that particular nation, state and society, although it is that most urgently and immediately.

Genocide is even more profoundly, as the Convention asserted, an 'odious scourge' from which mankind itself has to be liberated. Much attention has been given here to the repeated and fundamentally political unwillingness of the international community of nation states to fulfil their obligations to do so under the Convention. But as Bridget Conley-Zilkic and Sam Totten have pointed out, 'political will is generally the will to do something that is already determined. Perhaps the most serious gap is in political engagement ... something that we should demand of our governments, organisations and, foremost, ourselves'.[10]

How best to pursue this engagement is, of course, a matter of judgement for individual citizens, for the civil societies of which we are members, and for the states which govern us. It is an engagement, however, that is inevitable as we research and study genocide, as I have argued in this book; and it is one that, as citizens of the world, we may neglect at our peril. As Lemkin argued with such conviction and commitment, genocide destroys not only its immediate victims but, because it is aimed at the groups that make up humanity, attacks us all.

# Notes

## 1 Never again? From the Holocaust to the Genocide Convention

1 Raphael Lemkin, *Axis Rule in Occupied Europe*, Washington: Carnegie Endowment for International Peace, 1944.
2 Cited in John Cooper, *Raphael Lemkin and the Struggle for the Genocide Convention*, Basingstoke: Palgrave Macmillan, 2008, p.91.
3 Lemkin, *Axis Rule*, p.79.
4 See Anson Rabinbach, 'The Challenge of the Unprecedented – Raphael Lemkin and the Concept of Genocide', *Simon Dubnow Institute Yearbook* 4, 2005, pp.397–420.
5 These tensions are discussed in Rabinbach, 'Challenge' and also in A. Dirk Moses, 'Raphael Lemkin, Culture, and the Concept of Genocide', in Donald Bloxham and A. Dirk Moses (eds), *The Oxford Handbook of Genocide Studies,* Oxford: Oxford University Press, 2010.
6 Lemkin, *Axis Rule*, p.xi; p.79.
7 Ronnie Landau, *The Nazi Holocaust,* Chicago: Ivan R. Dee, 1994.
8 Cited in Samantha Power, *'A Problem from Hell': America and the Age of Genocide,* London: Flamingo, 2003, p.29.
9 See Richard Breitman, *What the Nazis Planned, What the British and Americans Knew,* New York: Hill and Yang, 1998.
10 See Tony Kushner, *The Holocaust and the Liberal Imagination: A Social and Cultural History,* Oxford: Blackwell, 1994.
11 See Donald Bloxham, *Genocide on Trial: The War Crimes Trials and the Formation of Holocaust History and Memory,* Oxford: Oxford University Press, 2001.
12 Cited in William Schabas, *Genocide and International Law – the Crime of Crimes,* 2nd edition, Cambridge: Cambridge University Press, 2010, p.40.
13 A detailed account of the drafting process can be found in Matthew Lippman, 'A Road Map to the 1948 Convention on the Prevention and Punishment of the Crime Genocide', *Journal of Genocide Research*, 4(2): 177–95.
14 *Prosecutor v. Kambanda*, Judgment and sentence, ICTR-97-23-S (4 September 1988), para.16.
15 Hannah Arendt, *Eichmann in Jerusalem – A Report on the Banality of Evil,* New York: Viking, 1965, pp.268–9.
16 Ibid, p.273.

## 2 The Genocide Convention

1 Florian Jessburger, 'The Definition and the Elements of the Crime of Genocide' in Paolo Gaeta (ed.), *The UN Genocide Convention – A Commentary*, Oxford: Oxford University Press, 2009.

2 See Robert van Krieken, 'Cultural Genocide in Australia' in Dan Stone (ed.), *Historiography of Genocide*, Basingstoke: Palgrave Macmillan 2008, pp.128–55.

3 John Quigley, *The Genocide Convention – An International Law Analysis*, Aldershot: Ashgate, 2006.

4 Martin Shaw, *What is Genocide?*, Cambridge: Polity, 2007.

5 See Norman Naimark, *Fires of Hatred – Ethnic Cleansing in Twentieth Century Europe*, Cambridge, MA: Harvard University Press, 2001, pp.185–98.

6 See Benjamin Lieberman, 'Ethnic Cleansing versus Genocide' in Bloxham and Moses, *Handbook*, pp.42–60.

7 William Schabas, 'Law and Genocide' in Bloxham and Moses, *Handbook*, pp.123–41.

8 See Elias von Sliedregt, 'Complicity to Commit Genocide' in Gaeta, *Commentary*, p.182.

9 See Katherine Goldsmith, 'The Issue of Intent in the Genocide Convention and Its Effect on the Prevention and Punishment of the Crime of Genocide: Toward a Knowledge-Based Approach', *Genocide Studies and Prevention*, 5(3): 238–57.

10 *Prosecutor v. Akayesu*, ICTR-96-4-T, para 519, cited in Schabas, *International Law* p.248. Schabas describes this as an 'isolated sentence', p.254.

11 Appeals Chamber in *Prosecutor v. Blaskic*, IT-95-14-A (29 July 2004), para. 694.

12 Jessburger, 'Definition'.

13 This is not, of course, to suggest that racism has disappeared. It can be argued that (partly as a result of Nazism) racism has been rearticulated, so that what were once seen as supposedly biological differences between groups have been recast as equally immutable cultural ones. See Kenan Malik, *The Meaning of Race: Race, History and Culture in Western Society*, Basingstoke: Palgrave, 1996.

14 Frank Chalk and Kurt Jonassohn, *The History and Sociology of Genocide*, New Haven, CT: Yale University Press, 1990.

15 *Jelisic* judgement, cited in David Luban, 'Calling Genocide by a Rightful Name – Lemkin's word, Darfur and the UN Report', *Chicago Journal of International Law*, Summer 2006: 303–20.

16 See David Nersessian, *Genocide and Political Groups*, Oxford: Oxford University Press, 2010.

17 Cited in ibid, p.106.

18 Cited in Nersessian, *Political Groups*, p.104.

19 See Caroline Fournet, *The Crime of Destruction and the Law of Genocide: Their Impact on Collective Memory*, Aldershot: Ashgate, 2007.

20 Beth van Schaack, 'The Crime of Political Genocide: Repairing the Genocide Convention's Blind Spot', *The Yale Law Journal*, 107(7): 2259–91.

21 Barbara Harff and Ted Robert Gurr, 'Towards Empirical Theory of Genocides and Politicides', *International Studies Quarterly*, 32(3): 359–71.

22 Benjamin Whitaker, 'Revised and Updated Report on the Question of the Prevention and Punishment of the Crime of Genocide', UN Doc. E/CN.4/Sub.2/1985/6.

23 Quigley, *International Law*, p.236.
24 Cited in Fournet, *Crime of Destruction*, p.75.
25 William Schabas, 'The *Jelisic* Case and the *Mens Rea* of the Crime of Genocide', *Leiden Journal of International Law*, 14(1): 25.
26 See Anja Seibert-Fohr, 'State Responsibility for Genocide under the Genocide Convention' in Gaeta, *Commentary*, pp.349–73.
27 Schabas, *International Law*, p.647.
28 Christopher Powell, *Barbaric Civilisation – A Critical Sociology of Genocide*, Montreal: McGill-Queen's University Press, p.72.
29 Barbara Harff, 'No Lessons Learned from the Holocaust? Assessing Risks of Genocide and Political Mass Murder since 1955', *American Political Science Review*, 97(1): 62. The figures for Guatemala are not confined to the genocide of 1982–3 (see Chapter 5). The figures for East Timor are from John G. Taylor, '"Encirclement and Annihilation" – The Indonesian Occupation of East Timor' in Robert Gellately and Ben Kiernan (eds), *The Specter of Genocide: Mass Murder in Historical Perspective*, Cambridge: Cambridge University Press, 2003. p.163. The figures for Chechnya are estimates from: http://www.instituteforthestudyofgenocide.org/oldsite/newsletters/29/ushmm.html, accessed 18 Sept. 2011. The figures for Sri Lanka are from the *Permanent People's Tribunal*, held in Dublin in January 2010, whose findings were published by the Fondazione Lelio Basso in Rome.
30 Gregory Stanton, available at: http://www.genocidewatch.org/aboutgenocide/8stagesofgenocide.htm, accessed 18 Sept. 2011.
31 William Schabas, '"Definitional traps" and Misleading Titles', *Genocide Studies and Prevention*, 4(2): 177–83.
32 See his introduction to the *Encyclopaedia of Mass Violence*, available at: http://www.massviolence.org/Our-scientific-approach, accessed 7 Nov. 2008.
33 Christian Gerlach, *Extremely Violent Societies – Mass Violence in the 20th Century World*, Cambridge: Cambridge University Press, 2010.
34 Patrick Wolfe and Henry Huttenbach, 'Responses to Christian Gerlach', *Journal of Genocide Research*, 9(1): 11–23.
35 Quigley, *International Law*, p.104.
36 See Schabas, *International Law*, pp.12–15.
37 David Scheffer, 'Genocide and Atrocity Crimes', *Genocide Studies and Prevention*, 1(3): 229–50.

## 3 Explaining genocide

1 Bloxham and Moses, 'Introduction', *Handbook*, pp.4–5.
2 Saul Friedlander: 'Trauma, Memory and Transference' in G. Hartman (ed.), *Holocaust Remembrance – The Shapes of Memory*, Oxford: Blackwell, 1994, p.259.
3 Leo Kuper, *Genocide: Its Political Use in the Twentieth Century*, Harmondsworth: Penguin, 1981, pp.57–8.
4 Helen Fein, *Genocide – A Sociological Perspective*, London: Sage, 1993.
5 Chalk and Jonassohn, *History*, p.23.
6 Israel Charny, 'Toward a Generic Definition of Genocide' in George G. Andropoulos (ed.), *Genocide: Conceptual and Historical Dimensions*, Philadelphia: University of Pennsylvania Press, 1994, p.76.

7  Benjamin Valentino *Final Solutions: Mass Killing and Genocide in the Twentieth Century*, Ithaca, NY : Cornell University Press, 2004, p.10; p.3.
8  Manus I. Midlarsky, *The Killing Trap: Genocide in the Twentieth Century*, Cambridge: Cambridge University Press, 2005.
9  Eric Weitz, *A Century of Genocide: Utopias of Race and Nation*, Princeton, NJ: Princeton University Press, 2005, p.236.
10 Robert Melson, *Revolution and Genocide: On the Origins of the Armenian Genocide and the Holocaust*, Chicago: University of Chicago Press, 1992.
11 Omer Bartov, *Mirrors of Destruction, War, Genocide, and Modern Identity*, Oxford: Oxford University Press, 2000, p.5.
12 Shaw, *Genocide*, p.33.
13 Martin Shaw, *War and Genocide – Organised Killing in Modern Society*, Oxford: Polity, 2003.
14 Once Soviet agreement had been secured, however, and with the onset of the Cold War, Lemkin then charged the Soviet regime with genocide on several occasions, largely it seems because he was trying (unsuccessfully) to use anticommunism to persuade the United States to ratify the Convention. See Anton Weiss-Wendt, 'Hostage of Politics: Raphael Lemkin on "Soviet Genocide"', *Journal of Genocide Research*, 7(4): 551–9.
15 See Michael McDonnell and Dirk Moses, 'Raphael Lemkin as Historian of Genocide in the Americas', *Journal of Genocide Research*, 7(4): 501–29; also John Docker's careful exposition of Lemkin's plans in 'Are Settler-Colonies Inherently Genocidal?' in A. Dirk Moses (ed.), *Empire, Colony, Genocide: Conquest, Occupation, and Subaltern Resistance in World History*, New York, NY: Berghahn, 2008, pp.80–101.
16 Lemkin, *Axis Rule*, p.79.
17 See Moses, *Empire, Colony*, p.15.
18 Dirk Moses, 'Conceptual Blockages and Definitional Dilemmas in the Racial Century: Genocide of Indigenous Peoples and the Holocaust', *Patterns of Prejudice*, 36(4): 7–36.
19 Jurgen Zimmerer, 'Colonialism and the Holocaust: Towards an Archaeology of Genocide' in Dirk Moses (ed.), *Genocide and Settler Society: Frontier Violence and Stolen Indigenous Children in Australian History*, Oxford: Berghahn, 2004, pp.49–76.
20 See the Special section: 'Genocide? Australian Aboriginal History in International Perspective', *Aboriginal History*, 25.
21 Krieken, 'Cultural Genocide'.
22 A. Dirk Moses, 'An Antipodean Genocide? The Origins of the Genocidal Moment in the Colonization of Australia', *Journal of Genocide Research*, 2(1): 89–106.
23 Patrick Wolfe, 'Settler Colonialism and the Elimination of the Native', *Journal of Genocide Research*, 8(4): 387–409.
24 Jurgen Zimmerer, 'Colonialism and the Holocaust: Towards an Archaeology of Genocide' in Moses, *Genocide and Settler Society*, pp.49–76.
25 Cited in Wolfe 'Structure and Event – Settler Colonialism, Time and the Question of Genocide' in Moses, *Empire, Colony*, p.115.
26 Wolfe, 'Structure', p.111.
27 Moses, *Empire, Colony*, p.23.
28 Moses, *Empire, Colony*, p.29.

29 Adam Jones and Nicholas Robins, *Genocides by the Oppressed – Subaltern Genocide in Theory and Practice*, Bloomington: Indiana University Press, 2009.
30 Adam Jones, 'Genocide: Ethical and Normative Perspectives' in Patrick Hayden (ed.), *The Ashgate Research Companion to Ethics and International Relations*, Aldershot: Ashgate, 2009, pp.215–32.
31 Mark Levene, *Genocide in the Age of the Nation State*, London: IB Tauris, 2008.
32 Powell, *Barbaric*, pp.148–9.
33 Powell, *Barbaric*, p.72.
34 Ben Kiernan, *Blood and Soil – A World History of Genocide and Extermination from Sparta to Darfur*, New Haven, CT: Yale University Press, 2007.
35 See Alexander Hinton (ed.), *Annihilating Difference: The Anthropology of Genocide*, Berkeley: University of California Press, 2002.
36 See Powell, *Barbaric*, p. 9; p.75.
37 Dirk Moses, 'Raphael Lemkin, Culture and the Concept of Genocide' in Bloxham and Moses, *Handbook*, p.22; 28.
38 Jacques Sémelin, *Purify and Destroy – The Political Uses of Massacre and Genocide*, New York: Columbia University Press, 2007.
39 Daniel Feierstein, *Genocidio como práctica social*, Buenos Aires: FCE, 2007.
40 Christopher Browning, *The Origins of the Final Solution – The Evolution of Nazi Jewish Policy, 1939–1942*, London: Arrow, 2005. See especially pp.309–14.
41 Hannah Arendt, *The Origins of Totalitarianism*, London: Allen and Unwin, 1958.
42 Zygmunt Bauman, *Modernity and the Holocaust*, Cambridge: Polity, 1989, p.92.

**4 Perpetrators, bystanders, victims and rescuers**

1 Raul Hilberg, *Perpetrators, Victims, Bystanders: The Jewish Catastrophe 1933–1945*, London: Lime Tree, 1993.
2 Bradley Campbell, 'Contradictory Behaviour during Genocides', *Sociological Forum*, 25(2): 296–314.
3 Irving Louis Horowitz, *Taking Lives: Genocide and State Power*, 4th edition, New Brunswick, NJ: Transaction Publishers, 1997.
4 http://www.hawaii.edu/powerkills/GENOCIDE.ENCY.HTM, accessed 25 Aug. 2011.
5 Moses, 'Conceptual Blockages'.
6 Michael Billig, *Banal Nationalism*, London: Sage, 1995.
7 On both armies and paramilitaries, see Alex Alvarez, *Governments, Citizens, and Genocide: A Comparative and Interdisciplinary Approach*, Bloomington: Indiana University Press.
8 Raul Hilberg, *The Destruction of the European Jews*, Chicago: Quadrangle Books, 1961.
9 Bauman, *Modernity*.
10 Powell, *Barbaric*, pp.15–16.
11 Robert Jay Lifton, *The Nazi Doctors: Medical Killing and the Psychology of Genocide*, London: Macmillan, 1986.
12 James Waller, *Becoming Evil – How Ordinary People Commit Genocide and Mass Killing*, Oxford: Oxford University Press, 2002, p.117.
13 Leon Goldensohn, *The Nuremburg Interviews – Conversations with Defendants and Witnesses*, (ed.) Robert Gellately, London: Pimlico, 2007.

136   *Notes*

14  Theodor W. Adorno and Daniel Levinson, *The Authoritarian Personality*, New York: Harper, 1950.
15  Arendt, *Eichmann.*
16  Christopher Browning, *Ordinary Men: Reserve Police Battalion 101 and the Final Solution in Poland*, Harmondsworth: Penguin, 2001, p.189.
17  Daniel Chirot and Clark McCauley, *Why Not Kill Them All? – The Logic and Prevention of Mass Political Murder*, Princeton, NJ: Princeton University Press, 2006.
18  Scott Straus, *The Order of Genocide: Race, Power and War in Rwanda*, Ithaca, NY: Cornell University Press, 2006.
19  Sémelin, *Purify.* See especially pp.41–3.
20  In Helen Fein, *Accounting for Genocide: National Responses and Jewish Victimisation during the Holocaust*, New York: Free Press, 1979.
21  Stanton, *8 Stages.*
22  Alexander Laban Hinton, 'A Head for an Eye: Revenge in the Cambodian Genocide', *American Ethnologist*, 25(3): 352–77.
23  Waller, *Becoming Evil*, p.290.
24  Ervin Staub, *The Roots of Evil – The Origins of Genocide and Other Group Violence*, Cambridge: Cambridge University Press, 1989.
25  Hannah Arendt, *The Origins of Totalitarianism*, London: Allen and Unwin, 1955, p.5.
26  Waller, *Becoming Evil*, p.235; p.120.
27  Staub, *Roots*, p.87.
28  Steven K. Baum, *The Psychology of Genocide – Perpetrators, Bystanders and Rescuers*, Cambridge: Cambridge University Press, 2008.
29  See Adam Jones (ed.), *Gendercide and Genocide*, Nashville, TN: Vanderbilt University Press, 2004.
30  Daniel Feierstein, 'Political Violence in Argentina and Its Genocidal Characteristics' in Marcia Esparza, Henry R. Huttenbach and Daniel Feierstein (eds), *State Violence and Genocide in Latin America – The Cold War Years*, London: Routledge, 2010, pp.44–63.
31  Baum, *Psychology*, p.89.
32  See, for example, the interviews conducted by Karen Monroe in *The Hand of Compassion – Portraits of Moral Choice during the Holocaust*, Princeton, NJ: Princeton University Press, 2004.
33  Samuel and Pearl Oliner, *The Altruistic Personality: Rescuers of Jews in Nazi Europe*, London: Macmillan, 1988.
34  See Jacques Sémelin, Claire Andrieu and Sarah Gensburger (eds), *Resisting Genocide – The Multiple Forms of Rescue*, New York: Columbia University Press, 2011.

## 5  Genocide during the Cold War

1  Robert Cribb, 'The Indonesian Massacres' in Samuel Totten and William S. Parsons, *Century of Genocide – Critical Essays and Eyewitness Accounts*, 3rd edition, London: Routledge, 2009.
2  Leslie Dwyer and Degung Samtikarma, '"When the World Turned to Chaos" – 1965 and Its Aftermath in Bali, Indonesia' in Robert Gellately and Ben Kiernan (eds), *The Specter of Genocide: Mass Murder in Historical Perspective*, Cambridge: Cambridge University Press, 2003, pp.289–306.
3  Ibid.

4 Robert Cribb, 'Unresolved Problems in the Indonesian Killings of 1965–96', *Asian Survey*, 42(4): 550–63.
5 Robert Cribb and Charles A. Coppel, 'A Genocide that Never Was: Explaining the Myth of Anti-Chinese Massacres in Indonesia, 1965–66', *Journal of Genocide Research*, 11(4): 474–65.
6 Robert Cribb, 'Political Genocides in Postcolonial Asia' in Bloxham and Moses, *Handbook*, pp.445–65.
7 Wardata Akmam, 'Atrocities against Humanity during the Liberation War in Bangladesh: A Case of Genocide', *Journal of Genocide Research*, 4(4): 543–55.
8 Mohammed Omar Farooq, 'Islam and Genocide: The Case of Bangladesh in 1971' in Steven Leonard Jacobs (ed.), *Confronting Genocide – Judaism, Christianity, Islam,* Plymouth: Lexington Books, 2009, p.139.
9 Geoffrey Robinson 'State Violence and Secessionist Rebellions in Asia' in Bloxham and Moses, *Handbook*, pp.466–88.
10 Donald Beachler, 'The Politics of Genocide Scholarship: The Case of Bangladesh', *Patterns of Prejudice,* 41(5): 490.
11 Cited in ibid, p.477.
12 Nicholas Wheeler *Saving Strangers – Humanitarian Intervention in International Society,* Oxford: Oxford University Press, 2000, p.58.
13 Suzannah Linton, 'Completing the Circle: Accountability for the Crimes of the 1971 Bangladesh War of Liberation', *Criminal Law Forum*, 21: 191–311.
14 Ben Kiernan, *Blood and Soil,* pp.158–60; 540–3.
15 Alexander Hinton, *Why Did They Kill? Cambodia in the Shadow of Genocide*, Berkeley: University of California Press, 2005, p.8.
16 Ben Kiernan, 'The Cambodia Genocide 1975–79, in Totten and Parsons, *Century,* p.346.
17 Ben Kiernan, *The Pol Pot Regime – Race, Power, and Genocide in Cambodia Under the Khmer Regime, 1975–1979,* 2nd edition, New Haven, CT: Yale University Press, 2002.
18 David Chandler, *Voices from S-20: Terror and History in Pol Pot's Secret Prison,* Berkeley: University of California Press, 1999.
19 Hinton, *Why Did They Kill?*
20 Alex Hinton, 'Oppression and Vengeance in the Cambodian Genocide' in Adam Jones and Nicholas Robins (eds), *Genocides by the Oppressed – Subaltern Genocide in Theory and Practice*, Bloomington: Indiana University Press, 2009, p.95.
21 Hinton, *Why Did They Kill?*, p.96.
22 Hinton, 'Oppression' p.97.
23 Power, *Problem*, pp.112–13.
24 Wheeler, *Saving*, p.96
25 Esparza *et al., State Violence.*
26 Daniel Feierstein, 'National Security Doctrine in Latin America: The Genocide Question' in Bloxham and Moses, *Handbook*, pp.489–508.
27 Victoria Sanford, '¡Si Hubo Genocidio in Guatemala! Yes There Was Genocide in Guatemala!' in Dan Stone (ed.), *The Historiography of Genocide,* Basingstoke: Palgrave Macmillan, 2008, p.565.
28 Victoria Sanford, 'From Genocide to Feminicide: Impunity and Human Rights in Twenty-First Century Guatemala', *Journal of Human Rights,* 7(2): 104–22.
29 Cited from interviews conducted by Jennifer Schirmer by Sanford, *¡Si Hubo!,* p.559. For a detailed analysis of the military's strategy, see

Jennifer Schirmer, *The Guatemalan Military Project: A Violence Called Democracy*, Philadelphia: University of Pennsylvania Press, 1998.
30 Cited in Valentino, *Final Solutions,* p.212.
31 Carlos Figueroa Ibarra, 'The Culture of Terror and the Cold War in Guatemala', *Journal of Genocide Research*, 8(2): 191–208.

## 6 Genocide after the Cold War

1 Martin van Bruinessen, 'Genocide of the Kurds' in Israel W. Charny (ed.), *The Widening Circle of Genocide*, New York: Transaction Publishers, 1994, pp.165–91.
2 See Kenan Makiya, *Republic of Fear: the Politics of Modern Iraq*, London: Hutchinson, 1989.
3 Human Rights Watch, *Iraq's Crime of Genocide: The Anfal Campaign against the Kurds*. New Haven, CT: Yale University Press, 1995, p.9.
4 Kurdocide Watch, 'Anfal': *The Iraqi State's Genocide Against the Kurds*, February 2011, accessed at www.kurdocide.com 24 April 2011.
5 Quoted in Said K. Aburish, *Saddam Hussein – the Politics of Revenge,* London: Bloomsbury, 2000, p.67.
6 *Iraq's Crime* p.8.
7 Ibid, p.xviii.
8 Bruce P. Montgomery, 'The Iraqi Secret Police Files – A Documentary Record of the *Anfal* Genocide', *Archivaria,* 52: 69–99.
9 Kurdocide Watch, *Anfal.*
10 *Iraq's Crime,* p.13.
11 See Mark Levene, 'Is the Holocaust Simply Another Example of Genocide?', in Simone Gigliotti and Berel Lang (eds), *The Holocaust – A Reader*, Oxford: Blackwell, 2005, see pp.434–6.
12 Michael J. Kelly, 'The *Anfal* Trial against Saddam Hussein', *Journal of Genocide Research*, 9(2): 235–42.
13 Naimark, *Fires,* p.168.
14 The Independent International Commission on Kosovo, *The Kosovo Report: Conflict, International Response, Lessons Learned*, Oxford: Oxford University Press, 2000, pp.301–13.
15 For a good survey, see Sabrina P. Ramet, *Thinking about Yugoslavia: Scholarly Debates about the Yugoslav Breakup and the Wars in Bosnia and Kosovo*, Cambridge: Cambridge University Press, 2005.
16 James Gow, *The Serbian Project and Its Adversaries – a Strategy of War Crimes,* London: Hurst, 2003, p.79.
17 Benjamin Lieberman, 'Nationalist Narratives, Violence between Neighbours and Ethnic Cleansing in Bosnia-Hercegovina: A Case of Cognitive Dissonance?', *Journal of Genocide Research*, 8(3): 307, n.1.
18 See Marko Hoare, 'A Case Study in Underachievement: The International Courts and Genocide in Bosnia-Herzegovina', *Genocide Studies and Prevention*, 6(1): 81–97.
19 Taylor Seybolt, *Humanitarian Military Intervention: The Conditions for Success and Failure*, Oxford: Oxford University Press, 2007, p.217.
20 Mahmood Mamdani, *When Victims Become Killers; Colonialism, Nativism and the Genocide in Rwanda*, Princeton, NJ Princeton University Press, 2001.

21 Mann, *Dark Side.*
22 René Lemarchand, 'The Burundi Genocide' in Totten and Parsons, *Century,* pp.483–504.
23 Robert Melson, 'Modern Genocide in Rwanda: Ideology, War, Revolution and Mass Murder in an African State' in Gellately and Kiernan, *Specter,* pp.325–38.
24 Christopher C. Taylor, 'Visions of the "Oppressor" in Rwanda's Pre-Genocidal Media' in Jones and Robins, *Subaltern,* pp.122–37.
25 Jean Hatzfeld, *A Time for Machetes – The Rwandan Genocide: The Killers Speak,* London: Serpent's Tail, 2005, p.53.
26 Straus, *Order.*
27 Linda Melvern, *Conspiracy to Murder – the Rwandan Genocide,* London: Verso, 2004.
28 Linda Melvern, *A People Betrayed: The Role of the West in Rwanda's Genocide,* London: Verso, 2000.
29 Daniela Kroslak, *The Role of France in the Rwandan Genocide,* London: Hurst, 2007.
30 William Schabas, 'Post-genocide Justice – A Spectrum of Opinions' in Phil Clark and Zachary D. Kaufman (eds), *After Genocide – Transitional Justice, Post-Conflict Reconstruction and Reconciliation in Rwanda and Beyond,* London: Hurst, 2008, pp.207–29.
31 Ibid.
32 Helen Hintjens, 'Post-genocide Identity Politics in Rwanda', *Ethnicities,* 8(1): 5–41.

**7 Genocide and humanitarian intervention**

1 See Nicholas Wheeler and Tim Dunne, 'East Timor and the New Humanitarian Interventionism', *International Affairs,* 77(4): 805–27.
2 Seybolt, *Humanitarian,* p.91.
3 Cited in Alex Bellamy, *Responsibility to Protect,* Cambridge: Polity, 2009, p.35.
4 Michael Barnett, *The International Humanitarian Order,* London: Routledge, 2010.
5 For a careful survey, see Alex de Waal and Bridget Conley-Zilkic, 'Reflections on How Genocidal Killings are Brought to an End', in Adam Jones (ed.), *Genocide – Sage Library of International Relations, Vol. 4,* London: Sage, 2008, pp.57–71.
6 See Matthew Krain, 'International Intervention and the Severity of Genocides and Politicides', *International Studies Quarterly,* 49: 363–87.
7 Bellamy, 'Military Intervention' in Bloxham and Moses, *Handbook,* p.601; p.616.
8 Report of the ICISS, http://www.iciss.ca/report-en.asp, p.vii; p.viii.
9 See James Kurth, 'Humanitarian Intervention after Iraq: Legal Ideals versus Military Realities', *Orbis,* Winter 2005: 87–101.
10 Bellamy, *R2P,* p.30.
11 See Mohammed Ayoob, 'Humanitarian Intervention and State Sovereignty', *International Journal of Human Rights,* 6(2): 81–102.
12 Powell, *Barbaric Civilisation,* pp.99–100.
13 See Stephen Werthheim, 'A Solution from Hell: The United States and the Rise of Humanitarian Interventionism, 1991–2003', *Journal of Genocide*

*Research*, 12(3–4): 161. But see also the sharp reply by Linda Melvern in 13 (1–2): 153–7.

14 Alan J. Kuperman, *The Limits of Humanitarian Intervention: Genocide in Rwanda*, Washington, DC: Brookings Institution Press, 2001.

15 Alan J. Kuperman, 'The Moral Hazard of Humanitarian Intervention: Lessons from the Balkans', *International Studies Quarterly*, 52: 48–9.

16 Leo Kuper, *Genocide – Its Political Use in the 20th Century*, New Haven, CT: Yale University Press, 1981, p.161.

17 D. J. B. Trim, 'Humanitarian Intervention in Historical Perspective' in D. J. B. Trimm and B. W. Simms (eds), *Humanitarian Intervention: A History*, Cambridge: Cambridge University Press, 2011, p.381.

18 Benedict Anderson, *Imagined Communities: Reflections on the Origin and Spread of Nationalism*, London: Verso, 1983.

19 Michael Walzer, *Just and Unjust Wars*, New York: Basic Books, 1977, p.101.

20 M. Byers and S. Chesterman, 'Changing the Rules about Rules? Unilateral Humanitarian Intervention and the Future of International Law' in J. L. Holzgrefe and Robert O. Keohane (eds), *Humanitarian Intervention: Ethical, Legal and Political Dilemmas*, Cambridge: Cambridge University Press, 2003, p.202.

21 See Eric Heinze, *Waging Humanitarian Law: The Ethics, Law, and Politics of Humanitarian Intervention*, Albany, NY: SUNY Press, 2009.

22 James Pattison, *Humanitarian Intervention and the Responsibility to Protect: Who Should Intervene?*, Oxford: Oxford University Press, 2010, p.154.

23 From Annan's address to the 2005 World Summit, available at: http://www.un.org/webcase/summit2005/statements/spenglsih3.pdf, accessed 12 Aug. 2011.

24 Thomas Weiss, *Humanitarian Intervention – Ideas in Action*, Cambridge: Polity, 2007, p.117.

25 Cited in John Hagan and Wenona Rymond-Richmond 'The Collective Dynamics of Racial Dehumanisation and Genocidal Victimisation in Darfur', *Sociological Review*, 73: 875; 893.

26 See Jennifer Trahan, 'Why the Killing in Darfur is Genocide', *Fordham International Law Journal*, 31(4): 123–33.

27 Scott Straus, 'Darfur and the Genocide Debate', *Foreign Affairs*, 84(1): 131.

28 Alex De Waal, 'Darfur and the Failure of the Responsibility to Protect', *International Affairs*, 83(6): 1039–54.

29 Mahmood Mamdani, *Saviors and Survivors: Darfur, Politics and the War on Terror*, New York: Pantheon Books, 2009.

## 8  Justice and prevention

1 Cited in William Schabas, *The UN International Criminal Tribunals – The Former Yugoslavia, Rwanda and Sierra Leone*, Cambridge: Cambridge University Press, 2006, p.604.

2 Donald Bloxham and Devin O. Pendas, 'Punishment as Prevention? The Politics of Punishing Génocidaires' in Bloxham and Moses, *Handbook*, pp.617–37.

3 Adam M. Smith, *After Genocide – Bringing the Devil to Justice*, New York: Prometheus Books, 2009, p.25.

4 Guénail Mettraux, *International Crimes and Ad Hoc Tribunals*, Oxford: Oxford University Press, 2005, pp.199–200.

5 William Schabas, *The UN International Criminal Tribunals: The Former Yugoslavia, Rwanda and Sierra Leone,* Cambridge: Cambridge University Press, p.185.
6 Mamdani, *Saviors,* p.284.
7 Bloxham and Pendas, 'Punishment'.
8 Benjamin N. Schiff, *Building the International Criminal Court,* Cambridge: Cambridge University Press, 2008.
9 Cited in Gary Bass, *Stay the Hand of Vengeance – the Politics of War Crimes Tribunals,* Princeton, NJ: Princeton University Press, 2002, p.13.
10 Mark Drumbl, *Atrocity, Punishment, and International Law,* Cambridge: Cambridge University Press, 2007.
11 Ernesto Verdeja, 'Institutional Responses to Genocide and Mass Atrocity' in Adam Jones, *Genocide, War Crimes and the West,* p.332.
12 Cited in Eric Stover and Harvey M. Weinstein, *My Neighbour, My Enemy – Justice and Community in the Aftermath of Mass Atrocity,* Cambridge: Cambridge University Press, 2004, p.303.
13 Fred Grunfeld and Wessel Vermeulen, 'Failures to Prevent Genocide in Rwanda, Srebrenica and Darfur', *Genocide Studies and Prevention,* 4(2): 221–37.
14 Barbara Harff, 'No Lessons Learned from the Holocaust? Assessing Risks of Genocide and Political Mass Murder since 1955', *American Political Science Review,* 97(1): 72.
15 Samantha Power, *A Problem from Hell: America and the Age of Genocide,* London: Flamingo, 2002.
16 The report was launched on 13 Nov. 2007. It is available at: http://www.ushmm.org/genocide/taskforce/report.php, accessed 25 Aug. 2011.
17 Daniel Feierstein, 'Getting Things into Perspective', *Genocide Studies and Prevention,* 4(2): 159. Emphasis in the original.
18 Martin Mennecke, 'Genocide Prevention and International Law', *Genocide Studies and Prevention,* 4(2): 177–83.

## Conclusion: the politics of genocide today

1 Scott Straus, 'A Step Forward', *Genocide Studies and Prevention,* 2009, 4(2): 185.
2 Available at: http://www.ushmm.org/genocide/about, accessed 25 Aug. 2011.
3 Helmut Anheier, Marless Kaldor and Mary Glasius (eds), *Global Civil Society 2005/6,* London: Sage.
4 See, for instance, Sanjeev Khagram, James Riker and Kathryn Sikkink, *Restructuring World Politics: Transnational Social Movements, Networks and Norms,* Minneapolis: University of Minnesota, 2002.
5 Jacques Sémelin has developed a very imaginative and innovative on-line *Encyclopaedia of Mass Violence* (http://www.massviolence.org). This is an electronic database, which includes maps and a steadily growing number of case studies, as well as theoretical papers.
6 Many of the key debates between historians are covered in the important collection edited by Dan Stone, *The Historiography of Genocide,* Basingstoke: Palgrave, Macmillan, 2008.
7 See especially the valuable set of essays on developments in several different disciplines in *The Oxford Handbook of Genocide Studies,* edited by

Donald Bloxham and A. Dirk Moses, Oxford: Oxford University Press, 2010. This work also covers a number of cases over a longer time span and even more continents than are covered here.

8 A particularly good example is the mix of academic analysis and eyewitness accounts in *Century of Genocide*, edited by Samuel Totten and William S. Parsons, London: Routledge, now in its 4th edition, 2012.

9 A pioneering work in this respect is the two volume set by Saul Friedländer, *Nazi Germany and the Jews vol 1: The Years of Persecution, 1933–1939*, New York: Harper Collins, 1997; *vol. 2: The Years of Persecution 1933–1945* London: Weidenfeld & Nicolson, 2007.

10 Bridget Conley-Zilkic and Samuel Totten, 'The Challenges of Preventing and Responding to Genocide' in Totten, *Century*, p.632.

# Appendix 1

**Articles I–IX From the Convention on the Prevention and Punishment of the Crime of Genocide**

Adopted by Resolution 260 (III) A of the U.N. General Assembly on 9 December 1948.
Entry into force: 12 January 1951.

The Contracting Parties,

Having considered the declaration made by the General Assembly of the United Nations in its resolution 96 (I) dated 11 December 1946 that genocide is a crime under international law, contrary to the spirit and aims of the United Nations and condemned by the civilized world,

Recognizing that at all periods of history genocide has inflicted great losses on humanity, and

Being convinced that, in order to liberate mankind from such an odious scourge, international co-operation is required,

Hereby agree as hereinafter provided:

**Article I:** The Contracting Parties confirm that genocide, whether committed in time of peace or in time of war, is a crime under international law which they undertake to prevent and to punish.

**Article II:** In the present Convention, genocide means any of the following acts committed with intent to destroy, in whole or in part, a national, ethnical, racial or religious group, as such:

(a) Killing members of the group;
(b) Causing serious bodily or mental harm to members of the group;
(c) Deliberately inflicting on the group conditions of life calculated to bring about its physical destruction in whole or in part;
(d) Imposing measures intended to prevent births within the group;
(e) Forcibly transferring children of the group to another group.

**Article III:** The following acts shall be punishable:

(a) Genocide;
(b) Conspiracy to commit genocide;
(c) Direct and public incitement to commit genocide;

144   *Appendix 1*

(d) Attempt to commit genocide;
(e) Complicity in genocide.

**Article IV:** Persons committing genocide or any of the other acts enumerated in article III shall be punished, whether they are constitutionally responsible rulers, public officials or private individuals.

**Article V:** The Contracting Parties undertake to enact, in accordance with their respective Constitutions, the necessary legislation to give effect to the provisions of the present Convention, and, in particular, to provide effective penalties for persons guilty of genocide or any of the other acts enumerated in article III.

**Article VI:** Persons charged with genocide or any of the other acts enumerated in article III shall be tried by a competent tribunal of the State in the territory of which the act was committed, or by such international penal tribunal as may have jurisdiction with respect to those Contracting Parties which shall have accepted its jurisdiction.

**Article VII:** Genocide and the other acts enumerated in article III shall not be considered as political crimes for the purpose of extradition.

The Contracting Parties pledge themselves in such cases to grant extradition in accordance with their laws and treaties in force.

**Article VIII:** Any Contracting Party may call upon the competent organs of the United Nations to take such action under the Charter of the United Nations as they consider appropriate for the prevention and suppression of acts of genocide or any of the other acts enumerated in article III.

**Article IX:** Disputes between the Contracting Parties relating to the interpretation, application or fulfilment of the present Convention, including those relating to the responsibility of a State for genocide or for any of the other acts enumerated in article III, shall be submitted to the International Court of Justice at the request of any of the parties to the dispute.

Text: U.N.T.S. (United Nations Treaty Series), No. 1021, vol. 78 (1951), p. 277.

# Appendix 2

## Organisations campaigning against genocide

Several organisations now exist which aim to raise awareness about genocide and to promote ways to prevent or halt it. These include:

*Genocide Watch*, set up by Gregory Stanton. This is the co-ordinating organisation of The International Alliance to End Genocide (IAEG), an international coalition of organisations (www.genocidewatch.org/).

*The Genocide Prevention Advisory Network*, which includes several distinguished genocide scholars, as well as diplomats, journalist and NGO activists (www.gpanet.org/content/gpanet-members).

*Genocide Prevention Now*, set up by Israel Charny, who did so much to make genocide a focus for study in the first place (www.genocidepreventionnow.org/).

*The Will to Intervene Project*, developed by Frank Chalk with General Roméo Dallaire and based at the Montreal Institute for Genocide and Human Rights Studies (http://migs.concordia.ca/W2I/W2I_Project.html). They have produced a very interesting study (*Mobilising the Will to Intervene: Leadership to Prevent Mass Atrocities*, Montreal: McGill-Queen's University Press, 2010) based on interviews with nearly 100 policy makers and practitioners involved in US and Canadian government decision-making at the time of the events in Rwanda and Kosovo.

*Gendercide Watch*, set up by Adam Jones, a project of the Gender Issues Education Foundation (GIEF), based in Edmonton, Alberta (www.gendercide.org/).

*The Genocide Prevention Project*, which came out of campaigns in the United States especially over the genocide in Darfur (www.preventorprotect.org).

*The Aegis Trust*, based in the UK and with strong links to Rwanda (www.aegistrust.org/).

# Glossary

**Anfal** Genocidal campaign launched by Saddam Hussein against the Kurds in 1988.

**Atrocity crimes** Umbrella term covering genocide, crimes against humanity, war crimes and the crime of aggression.

**Crimes against humanity** Offences which involve a serious attack on human dignity or grave humiliation or degradation, including murder, extermination, enslavement, deportation and forcible transfer, imprisonment, torture, rape and persecution.

**CEH** Commission for Historical Clarification, an enquiry in Guatemala into the genocide there.

**Eichmann Trial** Trial held in Jerusalem in 1961 by an Israeli court of Adolf Eichmann, one of the organisers of the Holocaust.

**Ethnic cleansing** Violent campaign to force an ethnic group out of a given geographic area.

**Gacaca** Form of justice used in Rwanda as an alternative way of dealing with perpetrators.

**IAGS** International Association of Genocide Scholars.

**ICC** International Criminal Court set up to try suspected perpetrators of genocide, crimes against humanity, war crimes and the crime of aggression.

**ICISS** International Commission on Intervention and State Sovereignty.

**ICJ** International Court of Justice which settles legal disputes between states.

**ICTR** International Criminal Tribunal for Rwanda.

**ICTY** International Criminal Tribunal for the former Yugoslavia.

**Janjaweed** Arab militias used to terrorise the population of Darfur.

**JNA** Supposedly the Yugoslav National Army, which effectively turned into the Serbian army.

**KLA** Kosovo Liberation Army.

**Ladinos** Term used to describe Guatemalans who speak Spansih, and identify themselves more as Western than indigenous.

**NAM** Non-Aligned Movement.

**NASAKOM** Term used by the Indonesian President Sukarno to denote the supposed fusion of nationalism ('Nasionalisme' in Indonesian), religion ('Agama') and communism ('Komunisme').

**Nuremburg Tribunal** The tribunal set up after the Holocaust to try leading Nazi war criminals.

**PACs** So-called 'civilian self-defence patrols' set up by the army in Guatemala, coercing peasants into attacking their fellow Mayans.

**Porrajmos** Term used to describe genocide of Sinti and Roma at the hands of the Nazis.

**PKI** Indonesian Communist Party.

**Politicide** Term coined by Barbara Harff and Ted Robert Gurr to cover mass killing of political groups (not covered in the Genocide Convention).

**RPF** Rwandan Patriotic Front, rebel army which invaded Rwanda and put an end to the genocide in 1994.

**R2P** Responsibility to Protect, new doctrine proposed by the ICISS and adopted by the UN in 2005.

**UNAMIR** United Nations Assistance Mission for Rwanda.

**USHM** United States Holocaust Memorial Museum.

**War crimes** Violation of the laws of war, including wanton destruction of undefended towns and villages, attacks on civilians, cultural institutions, plunder, collective punishment, terrorism, murder, rape, torture and slavery.

**WMD** Weapons of mass destruction.

# Index

post-colonialism 36; Serbian
83–84, 87, 89; and self-
determination 108; in
Yugoslavia 83
NATO 86, 89, 106
Nazism: and Fascism 15; and
genocide 1–4, 8, 27, 29–30, 86;
and Nuremburg Tribunal 4–5; and
omnipotence 38–39; and
perpetrators 45; and racism 14;
and Yugoslavia 83; *see also*
Einsatzkommandos, Holocaust
neo-imperialism 91
New Zealand 31, 71
NGOs 56, 115, 124–25
Nigeria 56
No Peace Without Justice 115
Non-Aligned Movement *see* NAM
North America 31, 128
Norway 71
Nuon Chea 69, 72
Nuremburg Tribunal 4–6, 17–18,
113
Nyiramasuhuko, Pauline 95

Omarska 84–85
Operation Searchlight (Bangladesh)
63
Operation Turquoise (Rwanda) 96

PACs (Guatemala) 53, 75–76
Pakistan 62–66
Pakistan, East *see* Bangladesh
Paraguay 107
Paramilitaries 29, 42–44, 123;
Serbian 87; Rwandan 94–96
Pattison, James 108
Pendas, Devin 116
Perpetrators 40, 101, 128; armies
and paramilitaries as 43; in
Bangladesh *see* Bangladesh;
bureaucrats as 44–45; and
bystanders 50–52; in Cambodia
*see* Cambodia; in Darfur *see*
Darfur; deterrence of 121;
emotions of 47–48; failure to
punish 113; and Genocide
Convention 11–14, 17, 26–27, 38,
127; in Guatemala *see* Guatemala;
and the ICC 127; individuals 117;

in Indonesia *see* Indonesia; in Iraq
*see* Iraq; and nationalism 37; and
omnipotence 39; personality of
45–46; post-colonial states as 126;
and process 48–50; prosecution of
56; punishment of 19, 20, 21, 116;
and rescuers 54; in Rwanda *see*
Rwanda; Serbia as 18; Soviet
Union as 35; states as 22, 41–42;
and truth commissions 118; and
victims 52; war on 119; in
Yugoslavia *see* Yugoslavia
Phnom Penh 67–68, 71
PKI 57, 59–60
Plan Victoria (Guatemala) 75
Pol Pot/Salon Sar/Brother Number
One 69–70
Politicide 16, 20, 122
*porrajmos* 1
Post-colonial states 36–37, 56, 61,
90, 105, 108
Powell, Christopher 20, 36–37, 105
Powell, Colin 111
Power, Samantha 123

Quigley, John 17

race 14–15, 25, 28, 34, 55
racism 34
Radio-Télévision Libre des Mille
Collines (Rwanda) 95
rape: as act of genocide 11, 21, 97;
in Bangladesh 64–65; in Bosnia
86; in Cambodia 69; as crime
against humanity 114; in Darfur
110; in Guatemala 74–75; in
Kosovo 86–87; in Rwanda 93;
*see also* sexual violence
*Razakars* (Bangladesh) 64
Reagan, Ronald 6, 76
reconciliation 97–98
reconstruction: as cause of genocide
38, 54; post-genocide 119
Regional Committee for the
Prevention and Punishment of
Genocide, War Crimes and
Crimes against Humanity 124
religion 16, 63, 69, 81, 84, 114
Republica Srpska 86
Republican Guard (Iraq) 80